GOD'S OWNERSHIP MEETS MONEY MANAGEMENT

HOW TO BE A GOOD AND FAITHFUL STEWARD

God's Ownership Meets Money Management

How to Be a Good and Faithful Steward

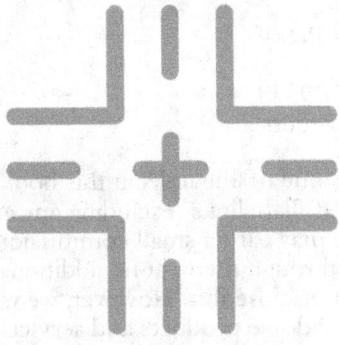

INTERSECTION

Where God's Wealth Meets God's Wisdom

JOHNNY MCWILLIAMS

Zero In Financial Press

Myrtle Beach, South Carolina

Zero In Financial Press
PO BOX 1718
Myrtle Beach, SC 29578
United States of America

Full Disclosure: Some of the links in this book and related
materials may be affiliate links (excluding any and all links to
Amazon), and we may earn a small commission when you
make a purchase through them, at no additional cost to you. By
FTC law we must disclose this. However, we want to assure
you that we only endorse products and services we believe in
and would or do use ourselves.

God's Ownership Meets Money Management, How to Be a
Good and Faithful Steward / Series: INTERSECTION,
Where God's Wealth Meets God's Wisdom / Johnny
McWilliams, author.

Hardback ISBN-13: 978-1-954485-11-2
Paperback ISBN-13: 978-1-954485-10-5
E-book (EPUB) ISBN-13: 978-1-954485-12-9
E-book (PDF) ISBN-13: 978-1-954485-14-3
Library of Congress Control Number: 2022909002

Access free resources mentioned in this book:
intersection.zeroinfinancial.com

Editor: Fleur Marie Vaz, fleurmarievaz@gmail.com
Additional Editing: Melanie Brown
Cover image design: Edgar Rios, edgrrr5@gmail.com

Contents

Dedication xi

Acknowledgments xiii

Free Downloadable Resources xv

Introduction - Fixing Your Focus 1

Part I: God Owns It All 7

    Chapter One: The Creation 9

        He Created the Heavens 12

        He Created the Earth 15

        He Created the Cattle and the Hills 18

        He Created You and Me 21

    Chapter Two: The Law 25

        The Owner Gets to Make the Rules 28

        Healthy Boundaries 32

        God's Wisdom Leads to the Good Life 35

    Chapter Three: The Redemption 43

        God Gave His Creation Free Will 44

        God Has the Right to Judge His Creation 47

        God Made a Way for His Creation 50

        God is in Control 52

Part II: Returning God's Portion 57

   Chapter Four: What Tithing Is and Is Not 59

      Not Giving. 62

      First and Best. 67

      Ten Percent 69

      Pursue Truth 74

   Chapter Five: Protection & Prosperity. 77

      The Most Significant Foundation Stone 81

      The First Line of Defense 84

      God Promises Prosperity 88

   Chapter Six: God's Examples 95

      Scripture Meets Nature. 97

      Jesus Reinforced the Tithe 103

      God Beat Us to the Punch 107

Part III: Being a Good Steward 111

   Chapter Seven: Working. 113

      Work Is Not a Curse. 114

      It's Tough But Good For You 119

      Laziness is Not a Gift 122

      Position In Your Purpose 126

   Chapter Eight: Learning 131

      Financial Degree from Proverbs 135

      Higher Education is Overrated 140

      Where Wisdom Meets Real Education 145

Chapter Nine: Managing.......................... 151

    Manage the Garden.......................... 153

    Investing What You Manage 158

    Entrepreneurship is Biblical 161

Chapter Ten: Money Management by
The Ten Commandments....................... 169

    THOU SHALT HAVE NO OTHER GODS
      BEFORE ME 170

    THOU SHALT NOT MAKE UNTO THEE
      ANY GRAVEN IMAGE..................... 172

    THOU SHALT NOT TAKE THE NAME OF
      THE LORD THY GOD IN VAIN 175

    REMEMBER THE SABBATH DAY,
      TO KEEP IT HOLY........................ 177

    HONOUR THY FATHER
      AND THY MOTHER........................ 179

    THOU SHALT NOT KILL 181

    THOU SHALT NOT COMMIT ADULTERY 182

    THOU SHALT NOT STEAL................... 184

    THOU SHALT NOT BEAR FALSE WITNESS..... 186

    THOU SHALT NOT COVET 189

Conclusion: The Greatest Commandments 193

Thank You to My Supporters! 199

Notes 203

About the Author 207

Dedication

I dedicate this book series to my Lord and Savior, Jesus Christ, who has carried me, walked with me, and led me all the way to completion. Thank You for always being the God who always keeps His promises.

> *And the Lord, he it is that doth go before thee; he will be with thee, he will not fail thee, neither forsake thee: fear not, neither be dismayed (Deuteronomy 31:8).*

Acknowledgments

I want to acknowledge and thank my best friend and incredible wife, Christine. Your undying support never ceases to amaze me. You have stood by me through it all. I couldn't have finished this project without you.

Thank you to my children, Seth and Paige. I love you and am so proud to be your dad. Your faith in Christ and success in life have been a beautiful display of God's grace.

Thank you to my parents, Clovers and Val McWilliams. You have always been a rock of consistent encouragement, believing in me throughout the decades. You both have faithfully studied the Word of God and have inspired me to do the same. Your prayers have kept blessings pouring out upon my life.

Thank you to my Pastor for over a decade, Al Toledo, for your powerful teaching and ministry that will always have a lasting influence on my business and writing. And to my current Pastor, Chris Honeycutt, who has been abundantly supporting as I worked through the last twelve months of this project.

Free Resources

To help you Zero In on the INTERSECTION where God's Wealth meets God's Wisdom, download the free resources from the INTERSECTION Resource Page:

intersection.zeroinfinancial.com

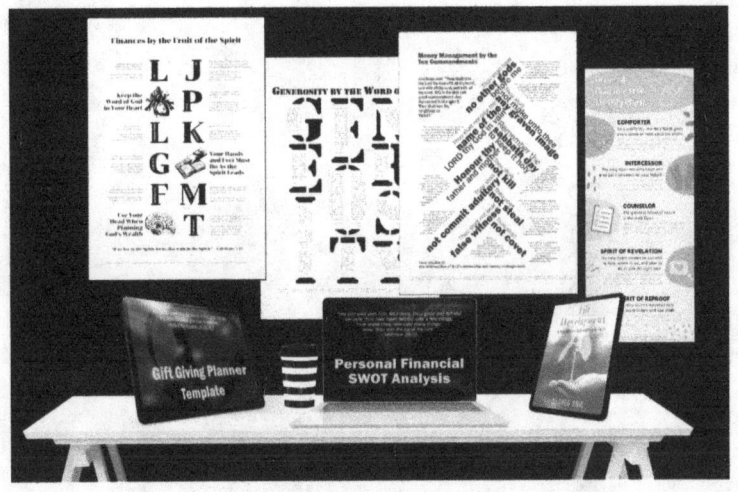

- **BOOK:** Life Development—A New Believer's Guide to Growing in Christ

- **INFOGRAPHIC:** Financial Guidance from the Holy Spirit

- **POSTER:** Finances by the Fruit of the Spirit

- **WORKBOOK:** Personal Financial SWOT Analysis

- **POSTER:** Money Management by the Ten Commandments

- **WORKBOOK:** Gift Giving Planner Template

- **POSTER:** Generosity by the Word of God

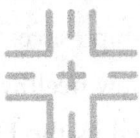

Fixing Your Focus

Twenty-nine years old, fresh out of bankruptcy, foreclosure, and repossession, I was broke and broken. "How did I end up here in this mess?" I asked myself as I lay in my uncomfortable U.S. Navy boot camp rack. "Where is my life heading?" I wondered, hoping this was the reset button I was looking for. It's funny how we never genuinely pray until we are at rock bottom.

Finally, as I cried out to God, I began to see more clearly. I realized that I was using God's wealth as if it were my own. What's more, I never looked to His Word and His Wisdom to guide me through life's ever-changing obstacle course. Though I never sought the Lord's guidance, I was quick to blame God when all my efforts failed. I finally asked myself a question worth asking: "If I am a child of God, why am I not acting like one?"

In *Biblical Faith Meets Financial Strategy*, you read how our radical relationship with God the Father, Son, and Holy Spirit is like no other connection on earth or in heaven. This relationship saves our souls, keeps us balanced, and helps us stay healthy amid life's many twists and turns. Jesus promised us the Holy Spirit, for example, so we would be confident and have power in all circumstances. This includes money.

I pray you made that decision presented in chapter one of *Biblical Faith Meets Financial Strategy*, to make Jesus your Lord and Savior. In case you missed it, I will include that opportunity in these pages. Also, review the section on financial guidance by the Holy Spirit and continually apply the principles of finances by the fruit of the Spirit.

That is only the tip of the iceberg, so to speak. Your relationship with God goes even further and deeper than you may realize. For a king's pride is in his children, those who have the responsibility to learn to manage his treasure for the kingdom. The King of kings wants nothing more than to give the whole earth to His children, and as a child of God, you have inherited and are tasked with managing a portion of the King's resources.

Once you become a genuine believer, you have access to the fullness of God. Biblical faith directs your financial strategy. In *Biblical Faith Meets Financial Strategy*, you see God as Savior, Father, Comforter, Reprover, Master, Intercessor, Counselor, and Revelator, directing our path with wisdom and love. Now it's time you see God the King and Owner of everything.

Welcome to *God's Ownership Meets Money Management*. The other books in this series are not a prerequisite for getting the fullness of these truths, so I'll quickly recap the premise of the series here.

In several applications, there is a pivotal tool known as crosshairs. You find this point of reference in sharpshooting and surveying, for example. The operator's scope has two engraved lines directing our focus when aiming at a target.

There is one reference for the horizontal plane and one for the vertical plane. The purpose is to align the crosshairs, where the two lines intersect, with the bullseye. Aiming to hit the bullseye requires precision, and using the simple principle of intersecting lines, you can easily pinpoint that target.

When peering through the scope of your financial future, there are several targets you should aim for. But, before you focus on the bullseye, you must ensure the crosshairs are zeroed-in or correctly calibrated to guarantee hitting your target.

The area that you must focus on is where the two lines intersect. In our case, those two planes are God's Wealth and God's Wisdom. Once you have these two crosshairs in focus and zeroed-in, you can aim right at the center of your target and hit it consistently.

This book series is for anyone who wants to understand the foundational principles of money. Each book is genuinely a one-size-fits-all because it reveals foundational principles instead of custom strategies. It doesn't matter your current age, wage, or stage. These are vital truths for every individual's financial life.

As a financial coach, I sit down and help people, face to face, and when they need a hug, shoulder to shoulder. It may be online or in-person, but in either case, my job is to listen, teach, and help guide them through a personal, tailor-made plan.

This plan is *their* plan, unique to their situation, goals, and aspirations. Zero In Financial® has a mission to help every client, reader, customer, follower, and fan zero in.

> *We will walk with you as you*
> *RECOVER from past money mistakes,*
> *GROW your present pocketbook position, and*
> *ZERO IN on your future financial fortune,*
> *ultimately leaving a lasting legacy of love.*

You need to RECOVER, GROW, and ZERO IN, all in your unique personal way. Although the strategy for each individual is customized, each must stay rooted in the same foundational principles found in the Word of God.

This book series will take you step by step through the foundational truths I use every day in coaching. Customization builds on top of these basic principles. Coaching is less about me talking and more about me actively listening. Everyone needs a mentor and coach, and I fill those voids as I encourage and guide. Even with the plethora of financial challenges you likely face, it comes down to the basics. When it's time to teach, this series is the playbook.

Again, if you want to pinpoint your financial destiny, you need to zero-in on your target, not someone else's mark. One of the most critical steps is to know where you are aiming. I will walk you through discovering your target, so you can zero-in with confidence.

You may have your financial target in sight but have yet to fix your focus. Have you ever heard the advice to fix your eyes on Jesus? That is expert advice and will surely do wonders for your financial plan. When you have the wrong perspective and have not fixed your financial plan according to God's Wisdom, you will miss the mark. You must manage God's Wealth with the proper point of view.

The blessings come where the two lines meet. It's time you have a focal point, so let's reveal the perfect intersection of God's Wealth and God's Wisdom for your life. If you are ready to be a faithful manager according to the Word of God, read on!

Part I

God Owns It All

CHAPTER ONE

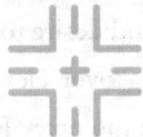

The Creation

When I was young, I was always a dreamer, wanting to start something or create something big! However, that didn't seem to impress too many. My teachers teased me in school for being seemingly unstable in my goals in life. There was always pressure to answer the question: "What are you going to be when you grow up?"

I had no definitive answer at the time. How could I when I was an innovator, a visionary, a creator in the wings? I didn't know how to describe my purpose yet, and entrepreneurship was never an option on the school's list of career aspirations.

When I went to college, I was always thinking way too deep about every assignment. My thoughts kept leaping ahead of the subject. Getting off track, not grasping simple concepts, I kept wondering how to disrupt ideas before I had a good understanding of them. My study habits were a mess.

After college, I could not hold down a job because I would easily get bored and desire to move on to something else. I remember having over eleven W-2s one February when preparing my income taxes for the year. Here I was trying to be an employee while stuck with an entrepreneur's mind.

I looked up to heaven and asked my heavenly Father, "What did you create me to be?" Asking this was vital because I recognized that I was not a randomly evolved mass of bones, organs, muscles, blood, and flesh that happened to come about by chance. Neither are you. Knowing that I am created with purpose, I decided to ask the Creator.

When I incorporated my first company at the age of 16, I was the owner because I began the business, filed the paperwork, and wrote the bylaws. I got to call the shots, and I got to reap the rewards and consequences of my decisions. There were more consequences than rewards, for I was young and dumb—all great lessons, nevertheless.

We don't often look at an enterprise and wonder how it came to be. There are listings of businesses, public and private, and a history of how each began. And believe it or not, every single one of them has a person, or team, who created it.

Let me illustrate. I took graphic arts in my last two years of high school. There I learned all about creative arts, from calligraphy to 3-D printing (which, at the time was cutting edge).

When I used the printing press, it outputted ink on a substrate. And when someone held the final product in their hands, they never wondered if there was a person behind the design. Every printed piece had someone who made it, and in this case, I was the pressman. And no matter how pretty or ugly, it always came out the way I designed it.

The same principle of design and process applies to everything in the business world. Every employer I've worked for has had rules and guidelines to go by, and as an employee I was expected to follow these policies. Also, there was a manager to oversee the work being done.

When I enjoy music at the Chicago Symphony Orchestra, I realize that every musician has a meticulously created set of notes to follow and a conductor is there to keep them playing harmoniously.

Every piece of art has an artist. Musical arrangements have a composer. Buildings have architects. Companies have an owner. The planets and stars, the heaven and earth, the plants and flowers, the mammals and fish, you and me, we all have a Creator: God.

So, who is the owner of Everything? God. Genesis 1:1 simply states: "In the beginning God created the heaven and the earth." If God created this company I am calling "Everything, Inc.," He is the owner, and He gets to call the shots.

Since you have certainly read *Biblical Faith Meets Financial Strategy*, I know you have committed your life to our Lord and Savior Jesus Christ. You have a personal relationship with the Father, the Son, and the Holy Spirit. Prayer and reading the Word of God is a part of your daily routine because of that relationship.

Now that your financial strategy is rooted in Biblical principles, and you have a financial plan solidified by the fruit of the Spirit, it's time you learn financial management according to the Creator's purpose.

He Created the Heavens

The Bible tells us all we need to know because it contains God's written bylaws for Everything, Inc. His vision script is there. He wrote the mission statement, partnership agreement, resolutions, meeting minutes, ... everything! Let's walk through the formation of the greatest organization ever.

The first verse of the Bible is pretty clear. I think even a first grader can understand this declaration.

The text continues to report what happened during the first few days of formation. The first day was busy as He created the heaven (notice it is singular) and the earth. I'll cover more about earth in a moment.

He created light (not to be confused with the Sun, which comes later) and He said that it was good. Then He made a distinction between light and darkness, calling light Day and darkness Night.

That was the first 24 hours of business formation, though God does not operate in the realm of time as we do. He created time for His creation. The Creator doesn't need time and lives outside of time. This concept blows our pea brains because He is God, and we are not. But, for our sake of reference, these events happened in a literal 24-hour span of time.

When creating a company in which the proprietor wants stakeholders to invest, they must explain some concepts in their head that the investors may not get. So, they describe it in terms that others can understand.

Steve Jobs, for example, had to figure out how to present a device that no one had ever seen and didn't even know they needed. He is quoted as saying about being an entrepreneur: "Our task is to read things that are not yet on the page."[1]

Many startups have the same predicament of how to translate abstract principles into simple words. But not God. The Bible beautifully presents the beginning of Everything, Inc. in a way that we all can understand. Let's continue.

"Now God created the firmament, and the firmament divided the waters from the waters." Whoa, what? So, the word firmament is defined as the sky or the heaven, and we see God called it "heaven" in Genesis 1:8. Also, notice that there is a separation of water; water below the firmament and, yes, water above the firmament.

God is a fantastic creator and a generous provider. You will soon see how His design was perfect for you and me to be prosperous and blessed beyond belief. But for now, just remember this water + heaven intersection.

Before I move on to the account of the world's creation, I would like to point out something easily missed. The Bible says God finished the "heavens" and the earth when the first week comes to a close in Genesis 2:1. You can do a study of this, and what you will find is that, ultimately, heaven was divided into three layers.

The first heaven is the sky, where the birds fly. The second heaven is space, where the planets and stars exist. And the third heaven is where you find the throne of God. Our finite mathematics and limited space telescopes could not even begin to calculate the vastness of the second heaven, let alone the beginning of the third heaven.

So, this water above the firmament, or heaven, is created most likely between the first and second heavens. (I will reveal the benefits of this later.)

King David in the Psalms even wrote a song about this part of the creation process. Here is an excerpt:

Praise ye the Lord. Praise ye the Lord from the
heavens: praise him in the heights ... Praise him,
ye heavens of heavens, and ye waters that be above
the heavens. Let them praise the name of the
Lord: for he commanded, and they were created
(Psalm 148:1,4-5).

Note that this Psalm was written thousands of years after these days of creation. Yes, creation is that important and impactful.

And, that is the end of the second day.

He Created the Earth

As I learned more about building a business and creating products, I understood the importance of sequential order—some objectives needed to be done before other tasks, even though they're all essential.

I've had no team members working for me during my many small venture creations. But when I do, I want to make sure that the history and formation steps that were taken are all intentionally documented. Someone should be able to look back and study the process that makes their company tick. There is purpose in the creation process, even though someone down the road may not understand why things are a certain way. But remember that the most loyal managers are the ones who understand the mind of the Owner.

Also, I learned some tasks depended on other tasks. For example, even though task-1 begins before task-2, task-1 may not be fully operational until task-2 is online. This is important when reading Genesis. You will notice God creating in a particular order, and there is a method to His mastery.

In the first two days, we have heaven and earth, and both have water. The earth is at this point without form and void, seemingly a fluid, unstable, and unoccupied sphere as described by the Hebrew word *tohu* (Genesis 1:2). So, the next natural step is to form the earth into something usable.

> *And God said, Let the waters under the heaven be gathered together unto one place, and let the dry land appear: and it was so. And God called the dry land Earth; and the gathering together of the waters called he Seas: and God saw that it was good. And God said, Let the earth bring forth grass, the herb yielding seed, and the fruit tree yielding fruit after his kind, whose seed is in itself, upon the earth: and it was so. And the earth brought forth grass, and herb yielding seed after his kind, and the tree yielding fruit, whose seed was in itself, after his kind: and God saw that it was good (Genesis 1:9-12).*

Now all the water gathers in one place and boundaries are put into place, revealing land not covered by the water where plants and trees start growing. I believe God ended the third day here for a reason. This process is documented to alleviate confusion and fake news many years later.

God wanted to make sure you knew that these were actual 24-hour days, not thousands or years. You see, plants won't survive years without sunlight and insects, and neither exists at this point. He knew there would be naysayers six thousand years later reading the Bible, so He made sure the creation story was solid. He accommodates the reasoning of scholarly fools.

Like I said, there are tasks that can begin before other tasks, but the first tasks may not be fully sustainable until the second tasks are in effect. Plants grew before they had the proper sustainable resources in place, leaving no doubt as to the length of a day. God is brilliant!

God formed the Sun, other stars, the moon, and the other planets on the fourth day. On the fifth day all the sea animals and creatures of the air were created. And He made all the land animals on the sixth day.

Before I go deeper, I would like to inspire you to go back and carefully study this entire process. As I mentioned in *Biblical Faith Meets Financial Strategy*, "There are more than 2,000 verses in the Bible about living the best life, utilizing all types of resources. There is everything from debt to budgeting to greed to work to riches to evil uses of money and everything in between."[2]

So, if you want to be prosperous and manage money well, you need to dig into all these truths. You will not only learn how to steward the Maker's resources, you will also gain wisdom in creating your own works of art, organizations, and inventions. We were created to be creators too. As the next sections presents, we were made in His image.

He Created the Cattle and the Hills

I'll get to the best part (the creation of you and me) in a moment. But first, I want to point out that God created everything perfectly. If we were to do a SWOT analysis on His startup, we would find all Strengths, no Weaknesses. All Opportunities were being maximized, and no Threats had a chance—that's 100% perfection.

God owns the cattle on every hill, and He maintains the hills. All living things were commanded to reproduce and multiply. He created the concept of exponential growth. We want our assets to appreciate, compound, and increase, so it would be wise to ask God to show us the way.

> *And God created great whales, and every living creature that moveth, which the waters brought forth abundantly, after their kind, and every winged fowl after his kind: and God saw that it was good. And God blessed them, saying, "Be*

fruitful, and multiply, and fill the waters in the seas, and let fowl multiply in the earth" (Genesis 1:21-22).

So, God's blessing initiates multiplication. Spoiler alert: when God commands us to multiply and fill the earth, He first blesses us. If you want the wealth you've been tasked to manage to compound, it would be wise to ask for His blessing. It is His to multiply, for He made and owns it all. **"The earth is the Lord's, and the fulness thereof**; the world, and they that dwell therein" (Psalm 24:1).

When a business owner is in the growth stage of business, she is proud of her creation. So, when the new hire challenges the firm's foundational principles, she may have to sit him down and have a talk with him. It is good to have all employees learn about the early days, so that they appreciate what they will be managing.

"Yours, O Lord, is the greatness, the power, the glory, the victory, and the majesty. **Everything in the heavens and on earth is yours,** O Lord, and this is your kingdom. We adore you as the one who is over all things" (1 Chronicles 29:11 NLT).

I think God is a proud creator of all that fills the earth. In the story of Job, I envision that meeting where God has to have "the talk" with him. Also, in this passage, we see that the dinosaurs certainly were living with humankind. Here is God describing the gigantic beasts roaming the earth in Job's time, which was probably around 2000 B.C.

"**Take a look at Behemoth, which I made, just as I made you**. It eats grass like an ox. See its powerful loins and the muscles of its belly. Its tail is as strong as a cedar. The sinews of its thighs are knit tightly together. Its bones are tubes of bronze. Its limbs are bars of iron. **It is a prime example of God's handiwork, and only its Creator can threaten it**.

"Can you catch Leviathan with a hook or put a noose around its jaw? Can you tie it with a rope through the nose or pierce its jaw with a spike? … If you lay a hand on it, you will certainly remember the battle that follows. You won't try that again! No, it is useless to try to capture it. The hunter who attempts it will be knocked down. And since no one dares to disturb it, who then can stand up to me? **Who has given me anything that I need to pay back? Everything under heaven is mine**" (Job 40:15-19, 41:1-2,8-11 NLT).

These are not mythological animals. They are real, and Job lived with them. God had to remind Job that He created everything with excellence, owns everything, and knows the idiosyncrasies of each creature intimately. If you read the entire book, you will see He used this opportunity to show Job that He is the Almighty Creator and a Father who loves him and will take care of him with all he could ever desire. All Job had to do was acknowledge God's might, humble himself, repent, and ask; this he ultimately did.

Give the Owner due respect. He is the Boss after all. As His prophet quotes of Him, "With my great strength and powerful arm I made the earth and all its people and every animal. I can give these things of mine to anyone I choose" (Jeremiah 27:5 NLT).

He Created You and Me

Okay, back to creation. He made man! Woo-hoo! It's the beginning of us! And, He made us in His image. "So God created man in his own image, in the image of God created he him; male and female created he them" (Genesis 1:27).

After each day of creation, God said that it was good. But, after He created us, He said it was "very good."

Then God did something extraordinary: He gave us the position of the manager. Adam and Eve were the perfect partnership, not just in marriage, but in business. God made all the animals, the birds, the sea creatures, the plants ... everything, for us to supervise.

And God blessed them, and God said unto them, Be fruitful, and multiply, and replenish the earth, and subdue it: and have dominion over the fish of the sea, and over the fowl of the air, and over every living thing that moveth upon the earth. And God said, Behold, I have given you every herb bearing seed, which is upon the face of all the earth, and every tree, in the which is the fruit of a tree yielding

seed; to you it shall be for meat. And to every beast
of the earth, and to every fowl of the air, and to
every thing that creepeth upon the earth, wherein
there is life, I have given every green herb for meat:
and it was so" (Genesis 1:28-30).

What an incredible creation! What an exceptional God! Today's earth is not like it was then, so I want to point out some fascinating things about the original masterpiece. There were some outstanding features at the beginning.

There was no death or violence at the start. You may have noticed that God told Adam and Eve that He had given them every green herb for meat. We didn't eat meat: every person and animal was vegetarian. We didn't use animals like we do today; I guess you could say we were vegan from the start.

God created all things to live forever! And animals and people didn't attack each other, nor were they afraid of each other. People could have cuddled up with a jaguar to take a nap back then. And one day, God will restore the earth to that state again. Read Isaiah 11:6-9.

Also, there were some massive animals, even dinosaurs. Plus, there were giant people once upon a time. Everything lived for hundreds of years. We have tons of archaeological evidence for all these things. If the Bible is to be taken at face value, these bones and artifacts are not millions of years old. What's up with that?

Now, remember that water above heaven? I believe there was some form of H_2O that divided the heaven from the heavens, just like the Bible says in Genesis 1:6-7. This would make the atmosphere radically different back then. When you consider this possibility, you end up with a creation made to flourish beyond our imaginations.

God created an atmosphere for growth, multiplication, prosperity, and limitless possibilities. And He wants that for you and me today. Don't worry; this is not a "get rich quick" plan. God's plan is a "work smart and reap the benefits" plan. And it wasn't exactly difficult, at first.

But what happened to the resistance-free, bountiful, prosperous environment that God created in the beginning? Let's dive into the answer to that question and explore many more financial truths in Chapter 2.

FREE DOWNLOADABLE RESOURCE

I suggested what a SWOT Analysis would look like if God was to access His work, but He is perfect and has no need for this exercise. But we should look at how we are doing and where we are going as we manage His resources.

There is a resource available to help you along on this journey of managing God's wealth with excellence. Download the *God's Ownership Meets Money Management SWOT Analysis* worksheet on the INTERSECTION Resource page: **intersection.zeroinfinancial.com.**

CHAPTER TWO

The Law

Parenting is not easy. Isn't that an understatement! But one of the duties we must carry out is making rules, applying those rules, and never wavering from those rules. When our children make a request, we give to them because we love them. But, if they ask for something we have already told them they could not have, what do we do?

A good child asks permission before she does something or goes somewhere. It is even wiser if she precedes the request with "May I...?" and concludes with "Please." Respect goes a long way though it does not guarantee we get our way. Even a good child asks for things she knows she is not allowed to have. But all children test their parents—some to the limit!.

God is a good and faithful Father as well as a fair and just Owner. He longs for us to come to Him with our requests, and this is one of the reasons for prayer.

Jesus assures us the Father hears prayers:

> *Or what man is there of you, whom if his son ask bread, will he give him a stone? Or if he ask a fish, will he give him a serpent? If ye then, being evil, know how to give good gifts unto your children, how much more shall your Father which is in heaven give good things to them that ask him? (Matthew 7:9-11)*

Asking for what you ought not have may not be the right thing to do, whether you are a child, or an employee, or praying to God. But, if the answer is still "no" and you do it anyway, be prepared for the necessary outcome. A good owner, boss, or manager will uphold the law, just as a good parent will enforce their rules. If they do not, there would be no respect for that authority.

Excuses are the great enemy of obedience. As a child, we convince ourselves that we know better than our parent. The employee decides that her way is better than the policy at play. "God didn't give us an answer," even though it is explicitly in His Word, is the common excuse to do it our way.

We may not always understand the rules. Every parent knows the one word that will most likely proceed from your son's mouth after telling him no.

"Why?"

"Because I said so..." we respond. And that is good enough.

As a good manager of God's Wealth, we need God's Wisdom, and that is more than good enough. I assure you that you will not understand God's way, God's timing, or God's plan all the time. But if you obey, there will be blessing and if you disobey, prepare for the necessary outcome.

As Moses declared the law to the nation of Israel, he gave them the following warning. We should take these words to heart and understand that God is the same yesterday, today and forever. When you respect the Owner, you should obey His Rules. This is just a subset of this passage of scripture. You will gain much wisdom if you go study it in its entirety for yourself:

"... **If thou shalt hearken diligently unto the voice of the LORD thy God, to observe and to do all his commandments ... all these blessings shall come on thee, and overtake thee**, ... Blessed shalt thou be in the city, and blessed shalt thou be in the field. Blessed shall be the fruit of thy body, and the fruit of thy ground, and the fruit of thy cattle, the increase of thy kine, and the flocks of thy sheep. Blessed shall be thy basket and thy store. Blessed shalt thou be when thou comest in, and blessed shalt thou be when thou goest out ... **But it shall come to pass, if thou wilt not hearken unto the voice of the LORD thy God, to observe to do all his commandments and his statutes which I command thee this day; that all these curses shall come upon thee, and overtake thee**: cursed shalt thou be in the city, and cursed shalt thou be in the field. Cursed shall be thy basket and thy store. Cursed shall be the fruit of thy body, and the fruit of thy land, the increase of thy kine, and the flocks of thy sheep. Cursed shalt thou be when thou comest in, and cursed shalt thou be when thou goest out ..." (Deuteronomy 28:1-6,15-19).

Obedience leads to Blessing.
Disobedience leads to Condemnation.

The Owner Gets to Make the Rules

As I pointed out, God, the Owner, and Creator of Everything, Inc., started it all. He gets the responsibility, and therefore gets to call the shots. He created the science of physics, chemistry, biology, zoology, astronomy, and every other (fill in the blank) -y. The expression "science is real" shortsights the truth: God is real, and He created science.

When God created everything, He also created the laws that go with it. We don't even understand gravity, but we must operate under the effects of gravity. If you try to break the law of gravity, there will be consequences.

There are also laws of wealth, and to go along with them, there are outcomes from obeying or disobeying. Like it or not, God said so.

If a business owner doesn't hold to what he says, his words will be worthless from now on. Suppose one employee fails a drug test, and there is a zero-tolerance policy, meaning the consequence is termination for failing a drug test? In that case, all the other employees will watch to see if the owner will fire this employee. Is he going to be a man of his word? Well, God is a Man of His Word. He does not lie or say one thing today and change it tomorrow.

God put Adam in the garden, so that means that God owns and gets to make the rules for Adam and the garden. Then He tells him he can eat from any tree. God gives Adam permission to consume from His provision.

But He then left man unambiguous instructions: "Everything is yours to manage, but this one tree, do not touch. If you break this law, you will surely die." Remember, our Creator made us with eternal life. Sin eroded many of the beautiful attributes of the creation. Disobedience brought death and violence into the world.

From the point when Adam and Eve rebelled, everything changed. Immediately, they did things and had feelings they had never experienced before. Fear—they hid, for they were afraid. Blame—they gave excuses for their actions. Lies—they were dishonest even after being caught red-handed (it must have been a tomato).

In that great decade of adventure, my twenties, I remember getting traffic tickets often. I would daily drive many miles, and I liked to speed. Soon I realized that speeding is breaking the law. If you are like me, you read that sentence and think, ha, the speed limit is a mere suggestion. But that is not true. It is the law.

I got pulled over many times, so many times that my driver's license almost got suspended. Every time the officer would ask me, "Do you know why I pulled you over?" I was not too fond of that question. He knew good and well that I knew I was speeding. But, for some reason, I would lie.

That's crazy, right? First, I break the law; then I lie about it. What a perfect example of our fallen nature today! The police officer might have had mercy on me if I had told the truth. But I will never know.

You hopefully shouldn't view your boss at work as a taskmaster but as a servant leader. Understanding her position, you should also know that there are rules for a reason, and they are there for everyone's good. Your company is most definitely not perfect, but God runs a flawless business.

God is not a dictator or tyrant; He never forces us to follow His law. He gives us freewill to decide and choose to obey. I will explore this in-depth by the end of this chapter.

As AnchorsAway puts it, "He is Sovereign and the King of Kings, but within His great mysterious plan for us, He has given us choice."[1] It is so amazing that our all-powerful God never imposes His will. He gives every manager an excellent model to use for running their operation.

We must continually read and study the rulebook, which is the Bible. All the answers are in there. I find it amazing that we forsake reading the Word of God and then wonder why we got into a financial jam.

Even the rulebook states that you should study the rulebook constantly.

"This book of the law shall not depart out of thy mouth; but **thou shalt meditate therein day and night**, that thou mayest observe to do according to all that is written therein: for then **thou shalt make thy way prosperous**, and then **thou shalt have good success**" (Joshua 1:8).

God, being the faithful, good, and just Owner that He is, always gives a promise that goes along with each law. Even in this command to Joshua, "meditate therein day and night," His intention is to ensure prosperity and success. Do you want to be prosperous? Look to the Bible. Is success your target? Read and meditate on His Word.

Just as importantly, "This book of the law shall not depart out of thy mouth." Yes! You need to speak these words of prosperity over your financial plan. Discuss God's holy principles with your family. Share the Word of

God with friends, family, coworkers, and neighbors. I am convinced that we are more than ever struggling today in money management because we have forsaken discussing the perfect financial principles and laws God has given us in this guidebook. Begin memorizing and communicating these truths, and watch them work.

The ball is in our court. As manager, we get to obey or disobey, follow His Word, or do it our way. The Owner gets to make the rules, and we get to decide whether we will abide by them. The choice is ours.

Healthy Boundaries

Why does God allow us to pay the price of sin? Why are we cursed when we disobey?

Because He loves us. As a parent, you dread punishing your children. But if you don't give them the penalty they deserve for their poor decisions, you will ruin them. You discipline your child because you love them.

Companies with the most loyal team members have guidelines that are upheld by management. Mark Williams, Director of Operations at BizFilings, states: "Work rules protect your business and your workers and, if correctly implemented and executed, create and maintain a better work environment for all."[2] He goes on to explain that fair policies maintain a high quality of work life for employees.

So, in short, the law and its ramifications are good for us. Rules keep our relationship with authority healthy. Discipline protects us from injuring ourselves.

"He that spareth his rod hateth his son: but he that loveth him chasteneth him betimes" (Proverbs 13:24).

Now I know today's parents don't discipline their children like they used to. Corporal punishment was still in effect in schools, and spankings were commonplace at home when I grew up. One of the many reasons children's behavior is so much worse today is that proper punishment is no longer in vogue. Pain works!

When you were a child, your parents taught you that there would be not so pleasant consequences for breaking the rules or disobeying. That makes you a better employee, a healthier citizen, and a respecter of authority. Without these critical lessons, people have realized what it looks like to have a society where laws are subjective. I describe it in one word: disorder.

Studies show that "failure to discipline children often results in kids who are unhappy, angry, and even resentful," as published on Very Well Family. The article continues, "… discipline is not about creating conflict with your child or lashing out in anger. Child discipline, when done correctly, is not about trying to control your child but about showing them how to control their own behavior … A child who has been taught right from wrong … will want to behave correctly out of a desire to be a good citizen and

As manager,

we get to obey

or disobey,

follow His Word,

or do it our way.

a member of their family and society—not because they fear punishment."[3]

Our loving Father in Heaven wants the best for us, just like any loving parent does. He instilled these psychological laws in us, and that is the reason they work. The law and the recognition that we broke the law drives us to repent if our hearts are right. God wants to move us to repentance and be reconciled with Him. He loves us and wants us to live in close communion with Him. If we love Him back, we show it by obeying.

Jesus said: "...If a man love me, he will keep my words: and my Father will love him, and we will come unto him, and make our abode with him" (John 14:23).

Boundaries are healthy. For example, we set up the rules and limits for the safety of our baby. Don't touch the stove. Keep your hands away from the electrical outlet. Stay inside the barrier that I set up. You don't want the baby to get hurt.

God continued to give us rules to follow throughout the entire Bible. All these laws are for our physical, mental, spiritual, and financial health, so we can live longer and enjoy the fellowship, monetary wealth, and experiences He has promised.

God's Wisdom Leads to the Good Life

God has given us the law to live by, not to control us. He has provided these laws to help us live the most prosperous life. The Ten Commandments are the foundational set of laws on which all the others are built. But, as you read through the Old Testament, you see humanity continually failing to keep the law.

"But wait, we no longer live under the law," you may exclaim. Paul, in Romans 3:31, answers that question: "Do we then make void the law through faith? God forbid: yea, we establish the law." One blogger explains: "The prime purpose of the Law is to expose our sinfulness and point us to faith in Christ's righteousness and when a sinner is saved by grace, **the Law has been established in that life**."[4]

Thank the Father who sent His Son to fulfill the law, for He is the only one to never break a single commandment. Jesus says, "Think not that I am come to destroy the law, or the prophets: I am not come to destroy, but to fulfil. For verily I say unto you, Till heaven and earth pass, one jot or one tittle shall in no wise pass from the law, till all be fulfilled" (Matthew 5:17-18).

Then what should we do with the Ten Commandments? What should we do with the entire Old Testament of the Bible? Is it all replaced by the New Covenant? If we do, we will fail to have the depth, richness, and unity of the "whole counsel of God" (Acts 20:27).

God is still God. We still read and study the Old Testament as a guide, having the understanding that we don't live under the law of Moses; but we now live by the "law of Christ" (Galatians 6:2). As Paul stated in Romans, the law has been established in our lives since we accepted Jesus as our Lord.

The law of Moses does not save us. Only Jesus saves. We no longer must communicate with God through a mediator like Moses or a priest, for now we have the Mighty Mediator and Highest Priest in Christ Jesus!

Praise God someone who commits murder today can accept Jesus into their life, be forgiven, and make heaven their home. Because we are all sinners and in desperate need of the Savior, this is great news!

If you have not made Christ the center of your life, I would like to invite you to pray a prayer of salvation. For anyone who believes and has faith will be saved from eternal death. I would love to invite you to join the family of God.

If you would like to know more and make heaven your home, go to salvation.zeroinfinancial.com.[5] There will be directions and next steps, plus a gift to help you learn more and grow as a Christian.

> **The gift I would like to send you is an indispensable resource. My dear friend, accountability partner, and fellow author, Pastor D. Greg Ebie has allowed me to distribute his book, "Life Development—A New Believer's Guide to Growing in Christ," to anyone**

who declares their life in Christ. I would like to thank him not only for writing this amazing book but also for allowing me to provide it to you.

I really wanted to share something that would help you grow your faith in Jesus Christ because Biblical Faith is the only way to develop a reliable Financial Strategy. Get ready to be challenged as you work your way through Pastor Greg's foundational guide.

Grab your copy of this study guide, and make sure to have your Bible at the ready! Download it today: salvation.zeroinfinancial.com[5]

After our relationship has been redeemed, we don't go back to our carnal ways, though. We are new creatures, born again, living for God and not for ourselves. As Harold Hancock writes, "The fact that the law of Moses, including the Ten Commandments, has ended does not mean that one can worship idols, take God's name in vain, disobey parents, steal, kill, commit adultery, or do other sinful things condemned in the Ten Commandments."[6]

So, we can still study these laws as foundational principles. The difference is today we have the Holy Spirit to help us resist temptation, and we have the blood of Jesus to cover all transgressions.

There are many laws in the Old Testament that were specific for that day and age. We can read them in context and see how their application for the time made sense, but we just don't use resources the same way as they did four thousand years ago. So, as you read the Bible, don't just gloss over scripture; study it, learn from it, and then apply it for today.

I've created a special resource named Money Management by the Ten Commandments. I pray you read it, study it, and be blessed by it as you apply these truths to your financial life. You can download, print, and post the PDF resource sheet, keeping it for reference in your office or home to help along the way. You can find this guide and this book series' free resources on this web page: intersection.zeroinfinancial.com.[7]

God's laws are not limiting; they lead to the good life. We saw how the first sin resulted in death. Just the opposite is true when you resist sin: the result is life.

When you intersect God's wisdom, which He shows us in His law, with God's wealth, which He freely gives us with principles to guide us, you find prosperity. His law includes advice, warnings, promises, and strategies.

In the next chapter, we will go deeper into this intersection, but here are a few examples:

God's Wisdom + God's Wealth in Genesis: "And I will make of thee a great nation, and I will bless thee, and make thy name great; and thou shalt be a blessing" (Genesis 12:2).

God's Wisdom + God's Wealth in Proverbs: "Labour not to be rich: cease from thine own wisdom. Wilt thou set thine eyes upon that which is not? for riches certainly make themselves wings; they fly away as an eagle toward heaven" (Proverbs 23:4-5).

God's Wisdom + God's Wealth in Matthew: "But when thou doest alms, let not thy left hand know what thy right hand doeth: That thine alms may be in secret: and thy Father which seeth in secret himself shall reward thee openly" (Matthew 6:3-4). [Alms is defined as, "money, clothes and food that are given to poor people"[8]]

God's Wisdom + God's Wealth in 1 John: "But whoso hath this world's good, and seeth his brother have need, and shutteth up his bowels of compassion from him, how dwelleth the love of God in him?" (1 John 3:17)

So, if you want to live the "good life," follow God's wisdom for sure. If you follow your way or the world's way, you end up with far less than what you could have had. Or, even worse, going against the law may cause extreme discontentment with wealth.

When I coach my clients to Zero In on their financial target, the first tool that we use is a budget. That is necessary because your financial plan sets "the law" and the boundaries for the money. It sets up shoulders on your wealth's road, so you don't run your financial vehicle into the ditch. A budget is not restricting; it is liberating. It allows you to freely spend and give, knowing that you are in a safe zone. Not wanting to budget is like hating lines on the street.

If you abide by God's law, you know you are in the safety zone. You don't worry and fret about every storm of life, like those without this liberty. The law gives you the freedom to work, play, and dream within these comforting limits. It's like walking along the shore just inside the line made by the crashing waves. You get to live the "good life."

CHAPTER THREE

The Redemption

The world is an unforgiving place. We live in a day when people cancel each other because of a mistake they made a decade ago. By contrast, God is unbelievably forgiving and patient, and we need to learn how to manage the resources He has given us in much the same way.

Also, I would like to reinforce some of the truths covered so far because the redemption of God's creation is a vital part of reclaiming our inheritance. Everything, Inc. was in deep trouble and the Owner of All came to the rescue. We must recognize how blessed we are and how much God loves us. I pray you realize that you have more to manage than you deserve, and you should not take it for granted.

God Gave His Creation Free Will

Our responsibility to choose right and wrong, good and bad, obedience and disobedience is ingrained in us. The Bible indeed shows us how making the right choices leads to prosperity and the wrong choices lead to hardship. This ability to follow God's wisdom directly affects the results we have with God's wealth.

From the beginning, we see God created everything, then gave Adam and Eve the free will to choose right from wrong. There was only one thing He commanded them not to do, and they went ahead and did it. And the penalty had to be enforced. They lost the richness of paradise because they could not resist temptation.

There are many examples in the Bible where the steward of God's resources chose to do what they ought not to do. One of the most chilling instances happened during the time of the first Christian church.

> *But a certain man named Ananias, with Sapphira his wife, sold a possession, And kept back part of the price, his wife also being privy to it, and brought a certain part, and laid it at the apostles' feet. But Peter said, Ananias, why hath Satan filled thine heart to lie to the Holy Ghost, and to*

keep back part of the price of the land? Whiles it remained, was it not thine own? and after it was sold, was it not in thine own power? why hast thou conceived this thing in thine heart? thou hast not lied unto men, but unto God. And Ananias hearing these words fell down, and gave up the ghost: and great fear came on all them that heard these things (Acts 5:1-5).

Before I understood God's ownership of everything, I didn't understand this passage. I didn't understand that He allows us to steward His resources for the good of ourselves, the church, and for others, and that God has laid out the law of right and wrong. I thought, "Was it not their land to do what they wanted with it?" And "Couldn't they change their plans if they wanted to?"

Then I realized they had promised to give the proceeds to the church as an offering. They had the free will to make that choice; but once they made that choice, they had to keep to their word.

The issue was that Ananias and Sapphira agree to lie to the church and say they sold the land they promised to give for a certain amount. Then they would keep the difference for themselves. They didn't have to make the promise, but they did. And then they followed that promise with a lie, cheating, and theft. If you read the entire story, you find out that Sapphira came in after Ananias had died. She, too, lied and suffered the same fate.

When you understand who owns it all and understand your place as a steward, you begin to use God's Wealth with God's Wisdom.

I don't know if that would happen to you if you did the same thing today. I don't want to find out either. The great economist Thomas Sowell says that "Greed is as constant as gravity,"[1] and he also exclaims that the constant erosion of moral values leads to destruction.

Many people cheat on their taxes, claiming to give to a charity a certain amount that was greater than their actual giving. I also know many others don't report all their cash tips, thinking that this will get them ahead. All these same people eventually struggle financially and wonder why.

We have a choice with all financial matters. It is never wise to cheat, commit fraud, lie, steal, or be a part of a scam, whether at work, in church, with the government, or concerning friends and family. Your foolish actions and lack of integrity will have consequences. That's the law put into place for our own good.

God Has the Right to Judge His Creation

One benefit of ownership of anything is that you can tear it down, rebuild it, or change it as you wish. Each of the houses that I have purchased has gone through modest renovations because I (or my wife) wanted to change the look of some room. But that was our prerogative.

The company that I own and operate today, Zero In Financial LLC, went by a different name, was structured differently, and has since been overhauled. This company is the same at its core, with the same mission, but there were modifications. Since I am the owner, I could make these alterations, and I didn't have to ask anyone for permission.

God owns everything. So you know what? He can flush it all if He wishes. Because He created the heavens and the earth and all that is within them, He can modify it, He can redeem it, and He can judge it. But He still gave humanity a choice.

The Bible says that He loves us so much He gives us time to repent. God gave those living at the time of Noah forty years to turn away from their evil desires. And even the cities of Sodom and Gomorrha had plenty of time to turn back to God. Today, we live in the last days and have the opportunity to accept Jesus Christ.

> *For if God spared not the angels that sinned, but cast them down to hell, and delivered them into chains of darkness, to be reserved unto judgment; And spared not the old world, but saved Noah the eighth person, a preacher of righteousness, bringing in the flood upon the world of the ungodly; And turning the cities of Sodom and Gomorrha into ashes condemned them with an overthrow, making them an ensample unto those that after should live ungodly ... The Lord knoweth how to deliver the godly out of temptations, and to reserve the unjust unto the day of judgment to be punished (2 Peter 2:4-6,9).*

God made us in His image, so we have an instinct for ownership and authority to build, manage, and decide as we see fit. We expect an investment fund manager to have the knowledge, the courage, and the ability to decide when to buy and when to sell. And we have no problem starting jobs, beginning businesses, and changing directions with our careers.

But as for God owning and operating His creation, many people are perturbed with how the world is run. I've learned not to question God. It is best to trust in His infinite wisdom. All the resources I have to manage have come from His hands, and if I trust He has only given me what He expects me to handle, I can believe He will provide me with the knowledge to go along with it.

If God influences one country's leader and takes authority away from another, it is His prerogative. Nothing happens by mistake if you believe God is in control.

This truth changes your perspective when it comes to job loss, or bankruptcy, or business failure. If you believe that you have free will and your decisions have repercussions, and God's judgment is always righteous, you are at peace with all circumstances.

Thinking of wealth building in this way is dramatically different from the norm. One may say it is radical, but I say it is the way it has been from the start.

God Made a Way for His Creation

God made a way out for us, and you know Jesus is The Way. We will only make the wrong choices over and over until we surrender to His Wisdom and His Word. Jesus is the Word that we need to follow. He shows us the way out of this crazy cycle.

The struggle is real. Look at what the Apostle Paul writes:

> *I have discovered this principle of life—that when I want to do what is right, I inevitably do what is wrong. I love God's law with all my heart. But there is another power within me that is at war with my mind. This power makes me a slave to the sin that is still within me. Oh, what a miserable person I am! Who will free me from this life that is dominated by sin and death? Thank God! The answer is in Jesus Christ our Lord. So you see how it is: In my mind I really want to obey God's law, but because of my sinful nature I am a slave to sin (Romans 7:21-25 NLT).*

Jesus is the way. The Holy Spirit gives you the power to overcome the sin nature. He came to fulfill the law because we cannot. Jesus is God's gift to redeem you from the consequences you rightfully deserve. Read Romans 8 to see what a wonderful gift this is.

So, we don't have to live legalistically, but the law still works as intended. Don't throw away your Old Testament. The words on those pages are not just good stories and reminders; they have principles by which to live.

Remember, Jesus says that He did not come to destroy the law but to fulfill the law. God is the same yesterday, today, and forever. The Old Testament remains relevant for us in so many ways. It is not suddenly okay to steal. Honoring your father and mother hasn't been canceled. And there is no Congress to veto God. His Word stands forever, and Jesus is that Word from the beginning. Study the Bible as you read, keeping the laws and stories within context.

As you put your life in the hands of God and surrender to the One who created the law and everything it governs, you will see fruitfulness like you have never seen before. Once you understand that when you are in control, the results are disastrous, you can release your life to live at the intersection of the cross. Where Jesus intersects the Law, there is liberty.

God fed the Israelites with manna from heaven in the wilderness of Sinai. Jesus said that He is the Bread of Life.

God provided water from the rock at Moses' command in Horeb. Jesus gives us Living Water and is the Chief Cornerstone from which that water flows.

Old: "And it shall be our righteousness, if we observe to do all these commandments before the Lord our God, as he hath commanded us" (Deuteronomy 6:25).

New: "But of him are ye in Christ Jesus, who of God is made unto us wisdom, and righteousness, and sanctification, and redemption" (1 Corinthians 1:30).

God made a way for us to be redeemed and live the dream. Though God's laws cannot be usurped, it's your choice to live by the world's standards or His. Choose wisely.

God is in Control

"Who hath saved us, and called us with an holy calling, not according to our works, but according to his own purpose and grace, which was given us in Christ Jesus before the world began" (2 Timothy 1:9).

At the beginning of this chapter, I walked through the process of creation. But I passed right through when describing the forming of heaven. Did you notice God created light, but He had not made the Sun or stars yet? From where was the light coming? I believe the light is coming from the Son. He wanted us to know from the beginning that He is the Light.

Jesus was there during the legal incorporation of Everything, Inc. He was there alongside the Father and the Holy Spirit the whole time. The Son is in control of it all.

"For by him were all things created, that are in heaven, and that are in earth, visible and invisible, whether they be thrones, or dominions, or principalities, or powers: all things were created by him, and for him" (Colossians 1:16).

"The Father loves his Son and has put everything into his hands" (John 3:35 NLT).

"Our lives are in his hands, and he keeps our feet from stumbling" (Psalm 66:9 NLT).

You don't have to fear when you are in the passenger seat, and Jesus is behind the wheel. It only becomes an issue when you try to take over the vehicle's destination. Trust the heavenly GPS (God Provides Sustenance).

There are no worries about politics and the stock market when you trust God for all provision and direction. You don't have to be concerned about your career while you are in tune with the purpose He has put inside your heart. As a child of God, you appear to be in control, but He is doing all the heavy lifting.

"And the Lord, he it is that doth go before thee; he will be with thee, he will not fail thee, neither forsake thee: fear not, neither be dismayed" (Deuteronomy 31:8).

If you watch the mainstream media, you will see the outcome of people not following their Maker. There are fears of climate change, famines, hurricanes, earthquakes, floods, volcanoes, and even asteroids, just to name a few. People are starving and desperately seeking solutions without seeking God to resolve their desperate straits.

But God says, "If my people, which are called by my name, shall humble themselves, and pray, and seek my face, and turn from their wicked ways; then will I hear from heaven, and will forgive their sin, and **will heal their land**" (2 Chronicles 7:14).

Where Jesus

intersects the Law,

there is liberty.

Blessing comes by the hand of God, and He has the authority to take it away. A prosperous life is only fruitful because the Lord has blessed your hand, your plan, and your land. God owns it all, and if you allow Him, He will flawlessly orchestrate everything. You only must humble yourself and wholly surrender.

There is a powerful example of the intersection of our surrender and God's provision in 1 Kings 17:8-16. It is the story of the Prophet Elijah and a widow God had instructed him to go meet, for she would provide him with food. Once at the widow's home, he challenged her to have faith and believe that God would provide for her and her son.

This story blows our mind because God had Elijah request this widow give up her last meal, the one she was clinging to for sustenance. There was a famine all around her home, and she could not see any way for her family to survive. This last meal was all she had.

She had to choose to obey and hope for a miracle, trusting that God would provide; or she could disobey and trust in her own plan. Did she trust God was in control? Yes, she did. And the result?

"And she went and did according to the saying of Elijah: and **she, and he, and her house, did eat many days**. And the barrel of meal wasted not, neither did the cruse of oil fail, **according to the word of the LORD**, which he spake by Elijah" (1 Kings 17:15-16).

God is undoubtedly in control!

Part II

Returning God's Portion

CHAPTER FOUR

What Tithing Is and Is Not

I love Genesis and the beautiful picture that is painted as God creates Everything, Inc. including His pride and joy: you and me. The fall and judgment that ensues clearly underscores The Owner as a good, fair, and just Creator; yet He makes a way for remediation. God loves us.

Throughout this story of the history of our glorious beginning and inglorious fall, we covered how laws were established to protect us, direct us, and help us prosper. As managers, we are given a free will but are expected to stay within the limits presented. Yes, we must prove our ability to manage, in the same way we do as an employee. We are

The most loyal managers are the ones who understand the mind of the Owner.

given proper responsibility just like a loving parent begins to allow their child to handle some chores and tasks that are age appropriate. God will not give you more than you can handle.

These laws are often confused as being religious laws instead of the righteousness of a right relationship. In *Biblical Faith Meets Financial Strategy*[1], I explain how the foundation of financial prosperity is rooted in radical relationship, not religion.

Tests that are in the form of financial boundaries are not set by a task master or there to limit your freedom. The Owner sets rules to keep the manager on track. The manager in turn obeys the rules trusting The Owner.

Respect and reverence are at the center of all healthy owner-manager relationships. We should not resent boundaries but should embrace them, knowing that they make us even more fruitful.

There are many tests at this owner-manager intersection, and there is no greater test than the tithe. The tithe was established since the beginning of time, before the law was ever written, as a foundational financial command. Though it wasn't labeled as "tithe" yet, it's been there from our world's conception.

In this chapter, you will learn where you can find this financial principle of tithing, what it is, and what it is not.

Not Giving

I know some terrific and well-meaning people who don't understand that the tithe is not an offering or a token of charity. An offering is a gift to show appreciation. Giving to charity and giving offerings are essential to include in a well-built financial house. Neither, however, belongs in the foundation.

You see, you don't give the tithe: you return the tithe. It belongs to God, but He allows you to have it in your possession. Now God wants to test you, just like He told Adam in the Garden of Eden, not to eat off "that" tree.

While offerings are optional, the tithe is not. God didn't say, "But if you get hungry and you just happen to be standing next to the tree of the knowledge of good and evil, and you are too lazy to stroll over to another tree ..." A command is a command.

The tithe is not an offering. The tithe belongs to God. Planning to tithe on purpose means not eating off that tree. Tithing is not giving. Rather, the act of tithing is giving back or returning what is not yours. These are two hugely different things.

The English language often befuddles me, and I can't imagine learning it as a second language. The word "give" is tricky. If I give someone a book, who owns the book? The person I gifted. Possession of the book switched from me to him, and I also passed along ownership. And by the way, it is important to note that giving the book was not an obligation.

If I ask to listen to a record album my neighbor has on vinyl and I tell her, "I will give it back to you tomorrow," then the next day I give it back to her, did I "give" her anything? Who was the owner of the LP the entire time, even when it was in my possession? She was. It would have been clearer if I said that I would "return" the record the next day, but it is more natural in English to say "give."

Maybe this difference is better expressed in other languages, but as I read the English translations of the Bible, I must understand the possibility of subtle nuances in a word like "give".

During a coaching session, I teach clients to Zero In on several financial targets, including Prayerfully Plan and Generously Give. Tithing belongs in the Prayerfully Plan category, not the latter. It is always first. The number one action I teach when planning the upcoming month's finances is to tithe off the top. When you pray, begin by thanking God for all that He has provided for you to manage; then return the tithe. While planning to tithe *on purpose*, place it at the top of the list.

The Bible speaks of tithes *and* offerings. When you give an offering, you are giving from the abundance God has blessed you with, as you Generously Give, whereas when you write that tithe check, you are returning God's sacred portion, as you Prayerfully Plan that abundance.

I don't want to beat a dead horse, but you may not have understood the importance of this pivotal and foundational cornerstone of personal finances.

Here are the two verses I am referring to concerning Adam in the Garden of Eden:

"And the Lord God commanded the man, saying, Of every tree of the garden thou mayest freely eat: But of the tree of the knowledge of good and evil, thou shalt not eat of it: for in the day that thou eatest thereof thou shalt surely die" (Genesis 2:16-17).

By the way, nowhere does it say in the Bible that you are going to hell if you don't tithe. This is not a salvation or sin issue; it's an obedience/love issue. Remember, this is a pivotal part of your relationship with your Creator and the Owner of all.

Tithing is not a religious rule, but a boundary God put in place for your own good. If you want to manage money from a position of strength, return the tithe. And if you stop or have never started tithing, your financial health will undoubtedly begin to die. God is a Man of His Word.

Because I have always kept meticulous financial records, even when not obeying Godly economic principles, I can go back and see a massive gash in my ledger. All of 2008 and half of 2009, I failed to return a grand total of $11,703. Now that I think about it, that means I made a lot of money in those 18 months. You would think I was doing well.

The reality was, I was holding back God's part—and that is never a good idea! This move was not honorable on my part. According to the computer software I used to track money matters, in January 2008, I was $27,000 in debt. By the end of 2009, I was over $80,000 in the hole. As you can see, tithing was not the only principle I was not applying.

By these numbers, I was not doing all that great in managing God's wealth. So much for the strategy of not tithing—a horrible error on my part! I quickly found out that touching the forbidden fruit comes with a curse.

But I also realized the evidence of blessing during my process of healing. From February 2010 to August 2010, I returned every penny of those tithes I kept.

First, this is not something required nor commanded by God. I only retroactively returned this money because the Holy Spirit commanded me to do this when I was praying about it, and I didn't want to be disobedient for a second time. It is always best to manage money as the Holy Spirit's prompting leads you.

Second, I am not rehashing this story to get a pat on the back or to show you how great I am. I believe this part of my testimony is for someone to hear, and I hope that person is you.

Now when I coach someone who is struggling financially, I am not surprised to find that they are not tithing. But, when my client begins or resumes tithing—

Step 1

Return the tithe.

Step 2

Pay your proper taxes.

Step 3

Budget the remainder.

with the right motives, which I will speak about in the following chapter—something miraculous happens.

The best thing I ever did was to continue tithing while finally deciding to get out of debt for good in 2015. My wife and I tithed as we tackled the mountain of debt that we had accumulated. We prayed, and we obeyed.

You would think that by using our entire God-given paycheck, we would demolish our debt load most speedily; but you would be wrong. It doesn't make mathematical sense—believe me, I know. Please know that I am a nerd, and I like stuff to add up. It didn't add up. Don't even try to analyze the tithe from a natural mindset; this is an established supernatural law.

All I know is, when you tithe with the correct point of view (even when you can barely make ends meet, or are trying to get out of debt, or trying to save up for something big), the rest goes further than the whole. I've seen it time and time again, and it still blows my mind every time.

First and Best

So now you see how The Creator gave the entire garden to Adam and Eve, instructing them to not touch His portion. Two chapters later, in Genesis 4, you will find another lesson on returning God's portion.

The children of Adam and Eve, Cain and Abel, were presenting gifts. Note, these were not regular offerings;

they were presentations (or the act of returning what is God's). God accepted Abel's sacrifice, and He did not accept Cain's. But why?

When it was time for the harvest, Cain presented *some* of his crops as a gift to the LORD. Abel also brought a gift—*the best* of the firstborn lambs from his flock. Cain's occupation was growing crops, so the fruit of the land was his paycheck, whereas Abel was a shepherd, so his increase came from animals.

Abel brought the *first and best* of his income, and Cain brought *some* of his income. Did you see how Abel brought the first and the best and Cain brought "some"?

I can't tell you how many times I thought paying my bills, going out to eat, saving money for later, and then returning the tithe was simply fine, later to find out that I was short that month. This shortfall is partly because of poor planning but also disobedience. A couple of verses later, God says this:

"You will be accepted if you do what is right. But if you refuse to do what is right, then watch out!" (Genesis 4:7a NLT)

Obedience is always the right thing to do, and in this case, it's returning the tithe. The right thing to do is to present to the Lord the first and the best of all He has blessed you with. John D. Rockefeller has been credited as saying, "I never would have been able to tithe the first million dollars I ever made if I had not tithed my first salary, which was $1.50 per week."

That verse in Genesis says to "watch out." But watch out for what? As you will see in the next chapter, the tithe is the first line of defense for the wealth that we must manage. It defends against life and hedges holistically. But watch out: when this defense is not in place, your financial plan will be exposed.

Also, think about this: if God didn't allow you to have the job or business you have, you wouldn't have it. Sometimes we can get cocky and think that we have what we have because we are so special. Not so fast, for it can all be taken away more quickly than you received it.

Last, we get confused with what "the first and best" refers to in our lives today and where it fits into the budget. Well, I'll cover that next.

Ten Percent

You may find many people who debate the size of the tithe. Up to now, we have discovered that the tithe is the Lord's, set apart and sacred. Also, we see it is first and best, so we could exchange the word tithe for the phrase "first fruits."

We use the word "tithe" because the answer to the question is within the meaning of the word. The definition of tithe is "tenth; broadly: a small part."[2] (Notice the word small.) This definition is in the third position in the Merriam-Webster dictionary. I wondered why it was so far down the list; then I realized an aged old fact: there will be opposition to anything rooted in the truth; hence it's somewhat buried.

The first definition is: "the tenth part of something paid as a voluntary contribution or as a tax especially for the support of a religious establishment." Can you see where the dictionary is confused? It gets the "tenth" part correct. But it says *voluntary*, which is technically right—you certainly have a choice. The problem is that there is a connotation that it is optional and for the benefit of the religious establishment. It also uses the word "tax," which most people would not consider voluntary but an obligation.

Ten percent is ten percent, not five percent, not 9.9 percent, not whatever you feel like this paycheck. Specifying the amount of the tithe is not legalistic; it is just a specific number.

"And **concerning the tithe** of the herd, or of the flock, even of whatsoever passeth under the rod, **the tenth shall be holy unto the LORD**" (Leviticus 27:32).

The tithe is not greater than ten percent either. I've read stories of people tithing 15%. As the Bible says, you can give an "offering besides," but the tithe is still the tithe. The amount above the tithe is a free-will offering.

Also note that, while you are still in debt, I advise you don't give substantial offerings or gifts until you are out of non-mortgage debt—unless God has told you to do otherwise. The offering is optional and beneficial for sure, but it is still not the tithe. God's design is perfect; there is no need to alter the blueprints.

Remember how I mentioned that a good entrepreneur documents the founding principles on which their company is built? That way, when someone down the road does not understand, they can learn. Well, the tithe is one of those truths rooted deeply in the foundation of managing God's Wealth with God's Wisdom.

So, how do you know if you have returned the first fruits? Use simple math and simple action.

Simple math, meaning, take your gross pay (Wage $20/hr, times 40 hours, Weekly pay $800), and move the decimal point over one spot to the left ($80). That's the first ten percent. Yes, before Medicare, Social Security, State and Federal Tax, and all those other mysterious deductions and contributions listed on your pay statement.

Then use simple action, meaning, write the check first (or send it online) before paying any other bills or buying other stuff.

Why is this so difficult to grasp? Super intelligent financial educators many times falter on this one. They may say, "It doesn't matter … gross, net, as long as you tithe." Say what? If you calculate taxes and other deductions and you pay tithe on what is left over, how would the tithe be first? I don't understand the confusion.

If you were interviewing for a job and they ask what your salary requirements are, is the number you give them gross (before deductions, contributions, taxes, etc.) or net (after all of the above)? If you were applying for a mortgage knowing that your approval is based on the amount of income, do you report your gross salary or net take-home-pay?

Why is it that we use our gross salary as the figure when it is most convenient for us, but as for the tithe, God gets moved down to the position below all the reductions on your pay stub?

These are all the questions the Holy Spirit asked me, and I had to decide for myself. I would like you to have that conversation with the Creator of Everything, Inc. for yourself.

I want nothing more than for you to hear those words: "Well done, good and faithful steward."

How do you know it's the best? Think about how you feel when you get paid and buy that first thing with that paycheck. For me, it was a Starbucks Upside-down Breve Caramel Macchiato with Extra Caramel. It's like, "Ahh, finally payday!" You have been waiting to get paid, and you celebrated getting the check (or direct deposit) with a treat or paying the bill that has been nagging you to death all week. Either way, it is the best.

However, if it was money spent before returning the tithe, it may later turn sour in your mouth. I bet when Adam and Eve bit into that fruit, it was the most fantastic tasting fruit anyone has ever tasted to this day. But the truth later came out, and they lost far more than they gained. It turned sour.

They had every other tree at their disposal! Think about that. You get to keep 90%. We can't complain. Now how the 90% gets managed and spent is a topic for another book. Or, even better, honing your budget can be a goal for a coaching session, since every household is unique. The point is, the first and best 10% is God's, and you get to decide what to do with the rest!

I think it is mind-boggling how God, the Owner of Everything, Inc., only requires 10%, and we, the managers, get to steward the remaining 90%. Yet sometimes we balk at this arrangement. Have you ever witnessed a company where the employees get 9 times more than the primary stakeholders?

And then, even worse, we hand over 15-30%, and sometimes more, of our income to the government with little hesitation. I realized the huge mistake of putting the government in the place of God in my finances. Don't fall for the same blunder.

So, where does tithing belong in your budget? The answer is: it really doesn't. I don't see taxes on most budgeting applications, and the tithe belongs in the position before taxes. So here's the correct order:

Step 1—Return the tithe.

Step 2—Pay your proper taxes.

Step 3—Budget the remainder.

Now, there are some budgeting systems that include the tithe, taxes, and other contributions before net pay. I am totally for this strategy because it makes you far more aware of every penny, making you a diligent manager. Most importantly, you should certainly budget every month with a tool and method you understand. I explain a simple 5-bucket methodology to create a powerful budget in an article[3] I wrote on my blog page Zero In On This.

Pursue Truth

Since we know the Bible is the source of all truth, we must ask: what does the Bible say about tithing? What is the truth? I will explore many scriptures which will expose the truth, but first I want to briefly define truth.

One of the most debated topics in the financial world is the tithe. There are debates as far as how much a tithe is. Some argue over the timing, in other words, when to tithe. Questioning even the reason to tithe happens all the time.

Some people have never even heard of the word. Others say it's an archaic biblical law. While others believe it's an optional principle.

It amazes me that there is a debate in the first place. But after contemplating the disagreements, I came to the same conclusion as when analyzing the dictionary definition: there will be opposition for anything rooted in truth. Human nature is such, it is easier to convince people to do something unhealthy than healthy. Discrimination is easy. Debt leads to fun. Eating food that is bad for you is delicious. At the start, these are all true.

But truthfully, it takes discipline to spend less than you make. Eating healthy takes motivation. Work is required when caring for your neighbor. And tithing takes self-control, intentionality, and love.

And in the end, making the human choices leads to discontentment, pain, and loneliness. In contrast, the bible-based decisions yield results of excellence.

So, as you can see, what is true is not always the "truth." In one of the commonly quoted passages of scripture, Jesus said: "...If ye continue in my word, then are ye my disciples indeed; And ye shall know the truth, and **the truth shall make you free**" (John 8:31-32).

The pursuit of truth is liberating.

Jesus is the Word, and Jesus is the Truth, and The Truth shall surely make you free. So, keep following Christ. And now that you know the truth, return the tithe, which is the Lord's, and then you will benefit from the subsequent financial blessing.

CHAPTER FIVE

Protection & Prosperity

It seems that my clients always want two things: protection and prosperity. Having unique goals, they are always in specific situations, and they all most definitely have some type of challenge. But, ultimately, no matter their walk of life, they yearn for protection and prosperity.

There are different words used to describe these common and natural human desires. Security is used to express the need for assurance that one's dreams will not be crushed by life and circumstance. Wealth is a word spoken to describe the building of something great that can be passed on from generation to generation.

Sometimes we look for insurance and savings to be at our defense. We use words like "security blanket" and "rainy-day fund" to describe the protection sought after. Some people use safety deposit boxes at their banking institution or large safes in their home, all to fulfill the need to safeguard.

Strategically Saving comes to mind when aiming for a prosperous future. Demolishing Debt is necessary because it is the gravity holding our prosperity from taking off. Some think that the road to success means working more and hustling to generate the most income possible. Everyone has a system or theory, all for their own unique financial dream.

These two important aspirations are not necessarily rooted in anything sinful, but I find that just the opposite is many times true. The desire for protection and prosperity has been downloaded into our DNA by God from conception. We come out of the womb wanting the protection of our loving parents and the room to stretch out, grow and prosper.

Think about your short-term financial goals. Personally, I know I want to be able to "move up" in car. That goal will obviously happen as I save the money to buy it, and that occurs only through prosperity. Also, within a week of making that purchase, I will be making another important purchase … insurance. Yes, you better believe this car will be protected! So, even our short-term goals are driven by the need for prosperity and protection.

Now imagine your financial life twenty years from now. I have never met one person who said that two decades from now they would like to be in the same financial situation that they are in today. Nope. They all wanted to prosper. Also, these same individuals and families were concerned with protecting their households, their retirement accounts, their businesses, their life.

If I want to achieve the ambition of leaving a perpetual scholarship fund after I die, I better become prosperous to fund such a dream. And a pile of wealth alone won't do; it needs to be protected and directed through a trust.

No matter what you desire to do, you need a plan of protection and prosperity. If you want to be an overseas missionary, you are going to have to raise the funds and make sure your plans are secure. Showing up in a foreign nation with no resources and no strategy is most likely going to end badly. Instead, you begin by doing what many who have gone before you have done: prosper and protect. There is no reason to reinvent the wheel.

Building your life and future and financial plan is just like the creation of a skyscraper. It starts at the bottom, the beginning, and the blueprint. The Bible has a lot to say about money, and it has a perfect plan for being prosperous and protecting. God gave us the blueprint.

So, if you want to manage the construction of your financial fortune without having to start over later—like I

Don't overlook the most significant financial foundation stone: The tithe.

experienced twice—you need to begin with the perfect plan. It all starts with the foundation.

The Most Significant Foundation Stone

I love looking at architecture and other beautiful structures around the world. Every time I've gone on an architectural tour in Chicago, Illinois, which has my second favorite skyline (sorry Chicago, but Hong Kong has you beat), I am amazed every single time. By going on an expert led tour, you get to experience things and see elements you would have never noticed on your own.

I'm always on the lookout for that one particular piece as a part of the foundation, the one element the guide will certainly mention: the building's cornerstone. This unique stone is often now a ceremonial or decorative element with the name, date of dedication and other important information. Placed on a prominent corner of the building, it is in clear view, though many times it's overlooked.

Once upon a time, the cornerstone was more critical. It began as the most important foundational piece of the structure. If you wanted to tear down an old stone building, just aim at the cornerstone, and everything else would fall.

According to an article on Britannica, "Until the development of modern construction, the stone was usually at a corner, possibly as the **first of the foundation**

stones, and it was a **real support** … From the original position and function of the cornerstone arose figures of speech in many languages referring to cornerstones or foundation stones of **character, faith, liberty, or other excellences.**"[1]

The cornerstone being first to be installed was sometimes referred to as the setting stone. For this essential piece supported all the other components of the structure. The other stones were reinforced because of this key piece.

In the book of Judges, there is the famous story of Samson, possibly the strongest man to ever live. In his last moments before death, he killed more of his enemies than at all other points of his life combined.

The way this came to be is by targeting the main pillars of the building in which there was a great fest of Philistines. Once again, Britannica states: "A pillar commonly has a load-bearing or stabilizing function",[2] just like the cornerstone. As Samson dislodged this chief support, the building's walls came crashing down, killing everyone that was present.

Therefore, you must pay the utmost attention to the most pivotal piece of any foundation. Jesus must be at the center of your life, for He is the Great Cornerstone. And in the foundation of your finances, the tithe must be the first stone laid.

The tithe supports all other financial activity. You must set it first at the top of your financial plan, even before the budget begins. It indeed strengthens your character and faith. All your financial walls need to be in alignment and the tithe should be the point where you begin. It is the most significant foundation stone.

In Genesis, we see God giving Jacob land. Notice, it is a gift to Jacob, and God says that it now belongs to him. "At the top of the stairway stood the Lord, and he said, "I am the Lord, the God of your grandfather Abraham, and the God of your father, Isaac. The ground you are lying on belongs to you. **I am giving it to you** and your descendants" (Genesis 28:13 NLT).

Now Jacob, being taught God's wisdom by his father and grandfather, knows that there is only one thing to do first with this wealth: return the tithe. "And this memorial pillar I have set up will become a place for worshiping God, and **I will present to God a tenth of everything he gives me**" (Genesis 28:22 NLT).

As I mentioned in *Biblical Faith Meets Financial Strategy*, surveyors use the crosshairs when planning construction. The coordinate in which the two crosshairs meet is the spot you are looking for; it is where you need to begin. The crosshairs of God's Wealth and God's Wisdom indicated that this is the point where you need to anchor your financial house and build: that's the tithe.

Just as with magnificent architecture, if you remove the most significant foundation stone, the building will tumble. I occasionally hear some exclaim, "I can't afford to tithe." Could you imagine someone saying to their architect, "The building plans look great, but I can't afford this main foundational piece! Just proceed without it." The thoughts that the architect would have in that moment are the same as I have about someone not being able to afford to tithe.

In our modern day, the cornerstone of a building is often overlooked. That is why the tour guide had to point it out. It is small compared to the rest. It is quietly doing its job, holding everything up, allowing its spectators to enjoy the grandeur of the structure it supports. Don't overlook the most significant financial foundation stone.

The First Line of Defense

The first place in the Bible turned to by most people concerning tithing is Malachi Chapter 3. Malachi 3:8-9 states: "Will a man rob God? Yet ye have robbed me. But ye say, Wherein have we robbed thee? In tithes and offerings. Ye are cursed with a curse: for ye have robbed me, even this whole nation."

So, here we see a warning *not to rob* God. To not return the tithe is theft. You will see later in this book that the law not to steal can be directly correlated to this command.

So, will something terrible happen if you don't tithe? As my testimony reveals, the curse is real. As you will see next, blessing and protection come with obedience. If you don't obey in this area, you will expose the wealth you are managing to the devourer.

When I think of that guy who said he could not afford to tithe, the truth is that it is not a matter of affording. When you realize it is not yours, it would be theft if not returned. It's the same as saying that you cannot afford to not steal from the grocery store, or you cannot afford to pay the proper amount of taxes due.

But here's the difference. The government needs us to send in those funds, supposedly, so they can provide services to the community (I will not get into what they really do with that money). God needs nothing from us. So, why is God so adamant that we return the tithe? Again, He placed this law to protect us and bless us. Don't stop with those few verses of Malachi; keep reading!

When I ask individuals how they protect their assets and possessions, they often refer to insurance first. Others mention their emergency fund as the first line of defense. But I want to teach you to Holistically Hedge. I want you to think of the tithe as the initial line the enemy of wealth must cross. Understand that God promises protection when you tithe.

> *"And I will rebuke the devourer for your sakes, and he shall not destroy the fruits of your ground; neither shall your vine cast her fruit before the time in the field," saith the Lord of hosts (Malachi 3:11).*

When someone goes through a financial hardship, sometimes it is not directly their fault. As some say, "Life happens!" But what if you can protect yourself from some of those difficulties in life? I have good news; you can! It's called tithing.

Security as a benefit of tithing is missed many times. The cornerstone has an aspect of protection for your financial house against the winds of life. If I may rewrite the story of *The Three Little Pigs*, I would say that the pig with the brick house was a tither.

Protection is a blessing and a promise from God. But as we now see, doing it our way and robbing God can lead to a curse. Looking back at Genesis, we can see this play out with Cain as he gave "some."

The Contemporary English Version reads, "If you had done the right thing, you would be smiling. But you did the wrong thing, and now sin is waiting to attack you like a lion. Sin wants to destroy you, but don't let it!" (Genesis 4:7 CEV)

You could read this verse and only see the negative side: if you do the wrong thing, you are cursed with a curse. But I want you to see the first choice as the only choice. I want you to be blessed. I will rejoice right along with you!

Last, we not only need to protect the wealth we are managing for God. We also need protection for the children God has blessed us with to whom we plan to pass this legacy. We can do that be teaching them how God owns everything, and that He has given us this commandment to return the tithe. By teaching our children to tithe from a young age, you will protect them from the devourer.

Satan was in the garden, lurking around to tempt Adam and Even to sin and touch the fruit set apart. Because of them disobeying, the curse was that there would be enmity, or a struggle, between the forces of evil and all humankind. We see our children targeted by the seed of the devil constantly.

I wonder if Adam and Eve told Cain and Abel the story of the first sin, the reason they had to pay the price of touching the first fruit. If they did, was Cain just making a choice against the wisdom of his parents? Was Cain being greedy in the moment, thinking that not returning God's portion would increase his prosperity? I don't know, but I know we can encourage and teach these truths to the next generation.

We can testify to the mistake of touching the first and the best, which is not rightfully ours. We can testify to the grace received once we obey. Let's use scripture and our personal testimony to impart blessing to the next generation. It will be the cornerstone of our legacies.

God Promises Prosperity

The tithe is a test, as we saw with Adam and Eve in the Garden of Eden. But here in Malachi, we discover God tells us to *test Him*!

God knew that there would be someone in the twenty-first century who didn't believe that it would be beneficial to return the first and best ten percent of their paycheck from driving Uber. So, He did something that He has never done for any other command or principle ever before and ever again. He tells us to put Him to the test. Yes, that's right; you can say to God, "Prove it!" Okay, please don't say it like that—but you get the point.

Let me present two different Bible translations of this verse:

The King James Version: "Bring ye all the tithes into the storehouse, that there may be meat in mine house, and **prove me now herewith**, saith the Lord of hosts, if I will not open you the windows of heaven, and pour you out a blessing, that there shall not be room enough to receive it" (Malachi 3:10).

The New Living Translation: "'Bring all the tithes into the storehouse so there will be enough food in my Temple. If you do,' says the Lord of Heaven's Armies, 'I will open the windows of heaven for you. I will pour out a blessing so great you won't have enough room to take it in! Try it! **Put me to the test!**'" (Malachi 3:10 NLT)

Wow! Just wow! What else can I say?

Robert Morris, in His book *The Blessed Life*, says, "Still unsure about this tithing business? Then take God up on the offer He makes in Malachi 3:10. ... God is essentially saying, 'Test me in this, I dare you!' ... That's why I want to extend a friendly challenge to you. Do the test! Begin to honor the Lord diligently with your first-fruits—the tithe—and see what happens."[3]

As I mentioned in Chapter 4, the principle of tithing with the correct mindset and heart had been the primary catalyst that God used for my family to get out of debt, become a good steward, and grow His wealth. We had been far from perfect, but God was so patient with us. He is faithful to His promises.

Obedience yields blessing. As you trust God to be faithful in His promises, you are not only blessed, but changed as you are obedient with the first fruits of His provision.

In Malachi 3:10, notice that it says to bring the tithe into the storehouse. Today, the storehouse is the local church where you are a member, not your favorite charity or a person in need. Don't give the tithe away. You need to return it to your church, not your uncle's friend's mom's church.

If you don't have a home church, find one. And if you can't see the need to go to church, read the third chapter of *Biblical Faith Meets Financial Strategy*.

I believe we have thousands of churches shutting down in America every year because people have not been obedient in this area. These organizations were feeding the homeless, housing orphans, taking care of widows, and improving communities. So, find a church that you can attend, serve, fellowship, and worship, and bring the first fruits with you. Blessings will follow, not just for you, but others too.

Also, this verse describes the blessing as so much that there will not be room enough for it. God wants to give you more than enough so that you will overflow with gifts for others. Your Father wants you to be blessed, but, more importantly, to be a blessing. Then He reaffirms, "And all nations shall call you blessed: for ye shall be a delightsome land, saith the Lord of hosts." (Malachi 3:12)

Finally, I want to present to you a novel idea. You may not like this idea at first, but promise to hear me out. Tithe by check.

I know filling out a check is a hassle. What a pain! And many of you may not even have a checkbook. (Note: I have a solution for that, order some.) I know, online payments are so much easier, with just a click of the button.

Friction makes you feel the money. It sets off the pain centers of the brain. Why would you want that to happen when tithing? So, you can think about the blessing that God had allowed you to manage. So, you can remember that it's not yours. So, reality hits home that God is giving you 90%, and you are returning His portion.

During the pandemic of 2020, we had to attend church online by watching service on YouTube because everything was shutdown. My wife and I had long been returning the tithe by check. Now we were using an online system for the first time in quite a while. It was so easy. I even had the thought: "Maybe we should just continue this after this is over." But then I remembered why we used checks for years.

When the offering basket comes around, I reach into my pocket to pull out the check. At that point, I feel it every time: God's grace. It is a moment of worship. I always say, "Thank You, Lord, for Your blessing that overflows in our life. Thank You, Lord, for Your hedge of protection. Thank You, Lord, for Your provision." I am filled with gratitude because when I look at that check, I remember God blessed us with nine times that amount to live on and give.

Then I remember to thank Him for the protection that He promises that comes with being obedient. "Thank You, Lord, for what I didn't have to go through or experience. Thank You for being a fence surrounding my family, protecting me from dangers I never have to realize."

The devourer is real! Don't forget to thank God you did not have to experience issues that were headed in your direction. You don't want to know about what you don't know about.

So, by writing a check and placing it in the offering plate, or basket, or bucket, or box, you feel that provision

**As you trust God
to be faithful in His
promises, you are
not only blessed,
but changed as
you are obedient with
the first and the best.**

and protection all the more. When you lose proper perspective, you lose productive prosperity. This way, by physically taking part, you won't forget how blessed you really are. Begin today and reap the benefits.

CHAPTER SIX

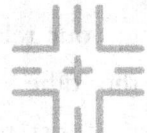

God's Examples

You can always count on a great owner to be a servant leader. What is the number one attribute of an effective servant leader? They lead by example. God demonstrates the tithe in nature, His Creation, through scripture, His Word, and by His own hand.

In this final chapter of Part II, I would like to bring to light these examples to reinforce this most important element of money management. Where the tithe may be an afterthought—if mentioned at all—in most Biblical-based financial books, I want to make sure you know that it is indeed the most significant foundation stone in your financial house. Without this essential piece in place, you will surely struggle with money management at best or completely fail at worst.

One word of warning, though. Tithing alone is not enough. I will expound on this later, but I want to point it out here. You must have a right relationship with your Creator.

It is worth repeating; your relationship with God is more important than the tithe. In fact, if you have dedicated your life to Jesus Christ, tithing will be merely an act of obedience. You won't have to worry about motive.

This is a warning because some have tried to tithe for the blessing that is promised without having a proper relationship in place first. Greed can grip out hearts. We can be in financial trouble, start tithing as if it's a quick fix, then blame God when our difficulties get worse.

Also, don't fall into the trap of tithing without yielding to the Holy Spirit in all financial matters. Go back and read the truths about financial guidance by the Holy Spirit in *Biblical Faith Meets Financial Strategy*. You must not only have the proper foundation in place but also have a sound structure when erecting the walls or placing the roof. Being faithful in one area doesn't give you a free pass in being faithful in every other area.

Check your heart as you place that check in the offering basket. Test your money mindset as you fill it out and enter the amount into your accounting system. Are you worshiping or worrying as you tithe? Worship is what we were designed to do. Worry indicates our misalignment.

We can get so caught up in the legalism of religion if we are not careful. I've caught myself half-heartedly tossing my tithe check into the offering basket as if I was saying, "Here God. I've done my duty." That is a sure sign of not being in the right spirit.

And relationship trumps religion every time. God loves you so much that He will provide for all your needs if you would just ask. And when we reciprocate that passion, we are acting in His image. He gives us a pattern to follow, and as you will see, tithing must be a natural outpouring of obedience, gratitude, and love.

Scripture Meets Nature

As we have discovered, God introduced the tithe at the beginning of creation to establish the most pivotal principle of this ownership/stewardship relationship. We see in Genesis 2:15, He used the tree as the object of His first fruits lesson. But what other lessons did the Creator infuse into His Creation?

Nature reveals one of these riveting examples: transpiration. I heard about this for the first time in a sermon series named *Like A Tree*.[1]

In this series, Pastor Al Toledo breaks down Psalm 1:1-3, teaching how we should be privately healthy to be publicly fruitful, just like a tree. Study these few verses. I promise, you will be blessed with specific actions you should live by so that you will be a blessing to others, live in your purpose, and prosper in all that you do. Here is the passage:

"Blessed is the man that walketh not in the counsel of the ungodly, nor standeth in the way of sinners, nor sitteth in the seat of the scornful. But his delight is in the law of the Lord; and in his law doth he meditate day and night. And **he shall be like a tree** planted by the rivers of water, that bringeth forth his fruit in his season; his leaf also shall not wither; and whatsoever he doeth shall prosper" (Psalm 1:1-3).

In the last message of Pastor Toledo's series, he explains transpiration:

> There is a very interesting thing about trees called transpiration ... When it rains, there is a certain amount of water that falls on trees. Trees and the forests act as the water pump of the world. ... There is a certain percentage of the water that goes right back up to the clouds. Actually, ten percent. That's funny because there is something in the Bible about ten percent too.

Yes, trees tithe. Biology Dictionary says, "As much as ten percent of the moisture in the Earth's atmosphere is from transpiration of water by plants." I think God is not only an incredible designer but is orderly in how he plans and teaches His principles. Nothing He has made and put into place is there by accident.

Pastor Toledo continues:

> *Rain falls from heaven onto the tree. The tree gives back ten percent. Water evaporates to the clouds on the coast and they bring it inland ... and then it falls on other trees ... [this pattern repeats over and over] ... Scientists have done studies in regard to rain fall all over the world. There is only one core issue: the presence of trees ... God has made it so that trees have this amazing ability to glean from the main source ... Without the presence of trees, after 400 miles inland it becomes desert.*

Trees return ten percent of the blessing of rain because God made it that way. This process creates a cycle of provision for other plants, animals, and all living beings. So, if we pattern ourselves after the tree, as the psalmist writes, we can partake in a continuous cycle of blessing, and "prosper in all we do." But what is the result when God's children are disobedient, or in nature's example, there are not enough trees? A desert.

According to Nonprofits Source—The Ultimate List Of Charitable Giving Statistics For 2018: "When surveyed, 17% of Americans state that they regularly tithe." And even though the statistics vary widely depending on the source, churches are financially struggling and closing all over America.

Trees return

ten percent of the

blessing of rain

because God

made it that way.

I'm sure there are many reasons for church closures, and the various complications are far outside the scope of this book and my knowledge. But I don't think these two facts are coincidental. There is undoubtedly a growing desert in America and all around the globe. What would happen if all of God's children used His Wisdom with His Wealth?

Don't say that you are too insignificant to make a difference. God will use you for His purpose. Remember that one of the tiniest seeds, the mustard seed, grows into one of the biggest trees. Be the tree you were called to be.

Before the Law, the tithe was established. We saw how the firstfruits principle was revealed in the Garden and with Cain and Abel. The first time we read of this principle being presented as a tenth is when the father of our faith, Abraham, gives a tenth of his wealth to Melchizedek.

> *And Melchizedek king of Salem brought forth bread and wine: and he was the priest of the most high God. And he blessed him, and said, Blessed be Abram of the most high God, possessor of heaven and earth: And blessed be the most high God, which hath delivered thine enemies into thy hand. And he gave him tithes of all (Genesis 14:18-20).*

Who is Melchizedek (also spelled Melchisedech in the Hebrew Bible and Melchisedec in the Greek), and why is

Abram giving him a tenth of his great wealth? Let's turn to the New Testament for more information:

> *For this Melchisedec, king of Salem, priest of the*
> *most high God, who met Abraham returning from*
> *the slaughter of the kings, and blessed him; to*
> *whom also Abraham gave a tenth part of all; first*
> *being by interpretation King of righteousness, and*
> *after that also King of Salem, which is, King of*
> *peace; without father, without mother, without*
> *descent, having neither beginning of days, nor end*
> *of life; but made like unto the Son of God;*
> *abideth a priest continually (Hebrews 7:1-3).*

Many Bible scholars believe that Melchizedek is Christ revealed once again in Genesis. This is one of many occasions you will read about a Bible character who must be Christ incarnate, i.e. appearing in bodily form.

The chapter in Hebrews even refers to Jesus as an Eternal Priest after the order of Melchizedek. I believe God placed this originating passage in the fourteenth chapter of the entire Bible for a purpose. It comes before the law; it reveals the Everlasting Priest and the King of Peace, and it solidifies the principle of the tithe.

It would be worth your while to do a deep study of Genesis 14 and Hebrews 7. There could certainly be volumes written about the parallels between Melchizedek and Jesus. I only want to show you how incredible, infallible and God-inspired the Bible is from cover to cover.

Jesus Reinforced the Tithe

Please do not cheat on your taxes. Do you agree with that statement? I hope so and for a good reason. Cheaters never win. When unfolding your financial vital signs in *Biblical Faith Meets Financial Strategy*, I present how to check your pulse for the mammon of cheating and stealing, amongst other conditions.

The same goes for the tithe, but ever more so. Do not cheat on your tithe, either.

With that said, the government will make you go back and pay all the back taxes you owe. But thank God, He is not a taskmaster like Caesar.

> *And they send unto [Jesus] certain of the Pharisees and of the Herodians, to catch him in his words. And when they were come, they say unto him, Master, we know that thou art true, and carest for no man: for thou regardest not the person of men, but teachest the way of God in truth: Is it lawful to give tribute to Caesar, or not? Shall we give, or shall we not give? But he, knowing their hypocrisy, said unto them, Why tempt ye me? bring me a penny, that I may see it. And they brought it. And he saith unto them, Whose is this image and*

> *superscription? And they said unto him, Caesar's.*
> *And Jesus answering said unto them, Render to*
> *Caesar the things that are Caesar's, and to God*
> *the things that are God's. And they marvelled at*
> *him (Mark 12:13-17).*

Jesus knew they were just trying to trap Him. But, He took this opportunity to teach them an imperative principle about ownership.

The tithe is for your good. Jesus recognized the importance of returning what doesn't belong to you. In another passage of scripture, we read Jesus explaining the tithe's importance in relation to other virtues.

As a side note, the New International Version translates "Render" as "Give back" showing that neither the tithe nor the tax is yours to keep. Other versions have the confusing English I mentioned earlier by using only the word "Give" which could be misconstrued as an act of giving.

"What sorrow awaits you teachers of religious law and you Pharisees. Hypocrites! For you are careful to tithe even the tiniest income from your herb gardens, but you ignore the more important aspects of the law—justice, mercy, and faith. **You should tithe, yes**, but do not neglect the more important things" (Matthew 23:23 NLT).

If you have children, you know what is best for them to do or not do. You are not trying to force them to do it, and you are certainly not trying to do them any harm. You want the best for your children, just like God wants the best for you.

That scripture above makes me remember when I saw a mother in the grocery store tell her son to grab a box of cereal from the end of the aisle. He heads in the direction of the breakfast section, knocking off things from the shelves along the way, runs over an older woman, and doesn't say excuse me. Did the son obey? Yes, but you know mom was furious. I'm sure she said something similar to what Jesus said. "Should you obey me and get the cereal, yes; but don't forget the important matters in life, like your manners!"

If your child disobeys you, how does it make you feel? Unloved? The same for God. "Wherever your treasure is, there the desires of your heart will also be" (Luke 12:34 NLT).

Do you love your child any less if they disobey? Nope. Same for God.

None of that changes the fact that you try your best to advise and guide your children towards the best things in life because you love them. None of that changes the fact that God instructs you and guides you toward the best things in life because He loves you.

Just begin tithing with your next increase (paycheck, dividend, commission, gift card, etc.) I promise you won't regret it.

Tithe out of love,

not obligation.

Intensely,

not begrudgingly.

Because of

relationship,

not religion.

God Beat Us to the Punch

I was always curious about where the idiom "Beat you to the punch" originated. It is a term that came from boxing; when someone got the first hit in, they "beat the other person to the punch." They essentially set the stage or passion for the rest of the match. If that first blow was huge, the other person would equal that effort; the competition was going to be intense.

This tithing principle is certainly not a fight or match with God. Let me be clear; our arms are too short to box with God. But God taught the principle for us to follow. He came out swinging; He came with intensity and passion. When He gave His first and His best, He went all the way.

Of course, I'm referring to Jesus, His First and Only Son. He gave us Jesus to redeem us from our sins, so that we may be saved and be home with Him throughout eternity.

I must refer to Pastor Robert Morris's book *The Blessed Life* once more, for he brilliantly speaks about this point.

> *Jesus Christ was God's firstborn Son, and He was born clean. He was born a pure, spotless lamb. But every one of us was born unclean; therefore, Jesus was sacrificed to redeem us. When He redeemed us by His sacrifice, He bought us back for God. He was literally a firstfruits offering. In a very real sense, Jesus was God's tithe. God gave His tithe*

> *(Jesus) in faith before we ever believed. Notice that*
> *God gave Him to us before we believed. Romans*
> *5:8 says: God demonstrates His own love toward*
> *us, in that while we were still sinners, Christ died*
> *for us. We have to give our firstfruits offering—our*
> *tithe—in much the same way. Before we see the*
> *blessing of God, we give it in faith.*[2]

There is no verse more frequently quoted than John 3:16. "For God so loved the world, that he gave his only begotten Son, that whosoever believeth in him should not perish, but have everlasting life." It is many times the first Bible verse someone commits to memory. This truth here is the most memorable Sunday School lesson I remember as a child.

To fully bring to light the awesomeness of this phrase "only begotten Son," I would like to look at the Greek word for "begotten," *monogenes.*

According to the Greek-English Lexicon of the New Testament and Other Early Christian Literature (BAGD, 3rd Edition), *monogenes* has two primary definitions. The first is "pertaining to being the only one of its kind within a specific relationship."[3] This is its meaning in Hebrews 11:17 when the writer refers to Isaac as Abraham's *only begotten son.* Abraham had other sons, but Isaac was the only son he had by Sarah and the only son of the covenant. Therefore, it is the uniqueness of Isaac among the other sons that allows for the use of *monogenes* in that context.

The second definition is "pertaining to being the only one of its kind or class, unique in kind." This is the meaning that is implied in John 3:16 (see also John 1:14, 18; 3:18; 1 John 4:9). John was primarily concerned with demonstrating that Jesus is the Son of God (John 20:31), and he uses *monogenes* to highlight Jesus as uniquely God's Son—sharing the same divine nature as God—as opposed to believers who are God's sons and daughters by adoption (Ephesians 1:5). Jesus is God's "one and only" Son.

So, God's first fruit is far greater than a mere ten percent; God gave His all. He loves us that much! I just want you to let that sink in and realize how much God gave us. Then, when you look at the measly tenth of our increase, it seems so insignificant. But, as we have seen in these three chapters, it certainly is not trivial to God. Again, the tithe shows our obedience and love.

You can do nothing to earn God's first fruit. It is free, and it is so unbelievably great. We don't deserve Jesus, the perfect Lamb of God, but Our Father redeemed us with His First, Only, and Best because He loves us. That's the powerful love of God in action. He beat us to the punch so we could follow with as much intensity as Calvary's cross revealed.

Following God's incredible example, I want to say, "I so love God that I return the tithe." Just purely out of love, not obligation. Intensely, not begrudgingly. Because of relationship, not religion.

It is that serious.

Part III

Being a Good Steward

CHAPTER SEVEN

Working

When I get on a call for a financial coaching session or an initial consultation, I always begin by praying. I know that if God is not involved, I don't want to be involved.

But, more importantly, I want to make sure the person or family on the other end of that call knows that they are managers of God's Wealth, and the best way to manage it is with God's Wisdom. As I've demonstrated, we tap into God's Wisdom through His Word and prayer. Furthermore, how could one be a great manager without direction from the owner?

The Merriam-Webster dictionary defines the word "steward" with phrases like: "a fiscal agent," and "one who actively directs affairs," and "manages domestic concerns."[1] Being a steward is a lot of responsibility!

Imagine being a restaurant manager, and you decide to spend the company's profits, remodeling the dining area, changing the menu, all without consulting the owner. That would be kind of crazy. You would probably get fired.

God has blessed you with many resources, and by making decisions without consulting the One who gave you the responsibility, you have done just the same.

Similarly, it would be absurd to be a lazy manager, expecting to remain in that position without working hard and giving it all you've got. There are supervisors and overseers with this detrimental mindset out there—but not you. You desire only to please the Owner of Everything, and make an effort to be the best steward you can be.

It's time to uncover how to be a good steward. And in this chapter, I want to begin by dissecting the concept of "work."

Work Is Not a Curse

Our Father in Heaven has created us to work. Work is not a curse or a punishment. God designed Adam with the desire to work. God mandated it to be so and instructed Adam to do so. During Genesis Chapter 2, we see a recap of some of the creation week, describing some of its events in more detail.

"And the Lord God planted a garden eastward in Eden; and there he put the man whom he had formed. And the Lord God took the man, and put him into the garden of Eden **to dress it and to keep it**" (Genesis 2:8,15).

Life was good for man from the beginning because God not only formed him in His image but gave him purpose and position. Adam had a job to do; he was there to tend to this beautiful garden.

The Creator, Owner, and Architect designed us to be productive. "For it is he that giveth thee power to get wealth" (Deuteronomy 8:18). Don't miss this incredible truth: God gave you the energy and ability to generate money!

As we see from the details of the six days of creation, God is a worker. It even says that God rested from His "work" on the seventh day, making this day holy. Even Jesus, who came to earth to seek and save the lost, worked as a carpenter. Paul, in addition to preaching the gospel, was a tent maker.

We need to work. Work gives us purpose. If you find a person who does no work, you will find a miserable person.

But it is necessary to rest too, just like God did during creation week. Show me a person who never takes one day per week to relax, and I'll show you a person who will eventually be on the brink of a physical and mental shutdown. If you want to earn more money, you must be more productive. If you want to be more productive, you must have a day of rest. God's formula works because He made it that way.

There are several other areas in life that are enhanced by work, but if not tended to, will fall apart. Family, fitness, faith, fun— just to name a few. Don't overwork even during the other six days of the week or there will be repercussions. Michael Hyatt writes, "We need to be equally concerned about the world outside of work. The truth is, if you don't, you won't be winning at work for very long."[2]

Monday mornings are not meant to be dreadful, and Friday evenings a relief. If you find it arduous to work a solid week, you need to seek God's will for your life by searching for the position that intersects that intention. God's purpose for your life will not be grueling.

Challenging is a different story. You will certainly have some tough days at work. These "weeds" in your work life are because of the curse, not because of the job. God created work for us in a perfect world, but after the fall, Adam and Eve's poor decision brought death and sin into the world, and with it came strain.

> ... *cursed is the ground for thy sake; in sorrow*
> *shalt thou eat of it all the days of thy life; Thorns*
> *also and thistles shall it bring forth to thee; and*

thou shalt eat the herb of the field; In the sweat of
thy face shalt thou eat bread, till thou return unto
the ground; for out of it wast thou taken: for dust
thou art, and unto dust shalt thou return (Genesis
3:17b-19).

At the start, God did not create work to be strenuous, and Adam did not have to sweat while keeping the garden. The garden could water itself, and there were no thorns and thistles. It kind of makes you wonder how great work was back then. It must have been thrilling.

Even today, this is a picture of what our Creator wants for us. We can't go back and reverse the curse; for example, you are still going to return to the dust. Nevertheless, I believe that the more you respect God's authority and word, and the more you resist disobedience and rebellion, the lighter work becomes. Work can be exhilarating once again.

Now that you realize God owns everything and knows everything, you know you have what you need to do, what He wills for you to do, and how He wants it done. Another way of saying this is, God has given you the perfect portion, the perfect purpose, and the perfect prescription. Here is the what, why, and how of work:

What: He has given you your **portion**, the exact amount of talent, money, and time you need at this moment.

God has given you the perfect portion, the perfect purpose, and the perfect prescription.

Why: He had given you a **purpose** in life. You are to use your portion for this purpose.

How: God gives you the **prescription**. His plan is perfect for you and never fails.

Now, apply His prescription towards your God-given purpose with your portion, and you will be in His perfect will.

It's Tough But Good For You

We see that even though work can be challenging, the work itself should be rewarding. It may be tough, but there are so many incredible benefits, and I would like to present three of them to you. "Be ye strong therefore, and let not your hands be weak: **for your work shall be rewarded**" (2 Chronicles 15:7).

First, work brings profit. Labor yields money, and the further you excel, the more you reap the benefits. For example, if you are in a trade, there are levels you can move up as your career progresses. There is a reward for your continued learning and diligence as promotion comes.

Hardly any entrepreneurial endeavor makes a ton of money in its first year. On average, it takes three to five years before the company is in the black. So, being a business owner is not for the fainthearted; it takes patience and persistence. But these go-getters can find some of the largest returns on their effort if they stick to it.

Homemakers get a bad rap these days because they are not earning a paycheck per se. But on the contrary, the one who stays home to teach the children, who handles the many chores, and manages the household is incredibly indispensable to so many lives. Many times, a homemaker allows their spouse to be the provider of that paycheck. When you are married and work on your purpose as a partnership, it is enormously effective.

The bottom line is that the benefit of earning currency is what can propel investing, giving, and living the dream. King Solomon, with all his wisdom, said, "In **all labour there is profit**: but the talk of the lips tendeth only to penury" (Proverbs 14:23). Yes, lip service results in extreme poverty, which makes intentional work even more beautiful.

Second, we can dedicate our work to the Lord. God created us to work, and when we are working within our purpose, we can make an impact. Your employment is on the right track when you have the satisfaction of knowing your work means something.

Some people can get caught up in working to cover tangible expenses like housing, food, and transportation. These necessities come from the income we receive, but God provided them through our skills, enterprise, and strength, etc. Thank God for all He gives, so we can focus on working for a higher purpose beyond the temporal.

Jesus used carnal thinking as a teaching moment. The people followed Him because He provided for their physical hunger. He said, "Labour not for the meat which perisheth, but for **that meat which endureth unto everlasting life**, which the Son of man shall give unto you: for him hath God the Father sealed" (John 6:27).

Yes, food is essential, but you work for something bigger. No matter what you do for work, you are being used by God for a purpose more significant than the paycheck. When you get to heaven, you will fully realize this benefit of work. Just remember, God achieves His purpose through your work.

Third, work brings joy, peace, and good health. There is nothing like going out, killing something, and dragging it home (metaphorically speaking). But really, our minds are geared to earn a paycheck, and our hearts are happy to be compensated for our efforts.

We love payday, and not just because of the money. There are even songs written about the joys of payday. I grew up playing board games centered on getting paid. There is even a candy bar by the name.

I mentioned already how we experienced the Covid-19 pandemic. One of the worst outcomes of this health crisis has been the government's response by shutting everything down for prolonged periods. Because of the shutdowns, many people lost their jobs, and some business owners had to close their doors forever.

In the United States, the federal government sent out stimulus checks throughout the summer to unemployed people. This help was additional money to the state's unemployment insurance payouts.

As some businesses reopened around the same time, an issue was made apparent. People were getting more money from these government agencies than they were receiving when they worked, so they didn't want to go back to work.

Now companies were having difficulty finding people to work, even though able-bodied people were sitting at home expecting their handout. However, these individuals' greed and slothfulness backfired on them as they got lazy and complacent. As studies indicate, "not working exposes us to an increased risk of additional illness and death."[3]

If only we would read our Bibles, we could avoid these mistakes. The Psalmist writes, "For thou shalt eat the labour of thine hands: **happy shalt thou be, and it shall be well with thee**" (Psalm 128:2).

Laziness is Not a Gift

While living in Chicago, Illinois, I realized how laziness has gripped many people to the point of being complacent. I'm sure this problem is not limited to that city but has infected communities all over the United States and throughout the world. The issue is that society has given them a crutch to lean on so that their work muscles have weakened.

I hear it all the time, how their neighborhood is the fault they can't work, or their family situation is the culprit, or, the worst is using race or gender as the excuse for not rising to the occasion. Laziness can result from a limiting belief shaping one's emotions and mental state. So, watch out!

Are there legit weeds in the garden of life? Yes, all the time, and there always will be. But the more you tell someone that they can't overcome, the more likely they won't. Praise God that in America, we all have opportunities to rise above our current situations in life. Don't use societal lies as an excuse to not work to your fullest for God's glory.

Dr. Carol Swain, former university professor of political science and law, author and editor of several books, and a nationally known political commentator and podcast host, writes:

> *Here are some life lessons I learned from my journey from rural poverty to success as a tenured professor at Vanderbilt and Princeton universities, and now as a public intellectual:*
> - *Everyone has the potential to overcome life's disadvantages.*
> - *Where you start your life does not determine where you end up.*
> - *Your attitude toward life, and what you believe about reality, are far more important than your race, gender, or*

social class in determining what you will accomplish in life.

- *Everyone is unique. If you do your part with what God has tasked you to manage, He will do the rest.*[4]

There are many alerts in scripture about the enemies of work. Warnings about laziness are throughout all the Word. You could do a lifelong Bible study just on this one warning concerning improper work (or lack thereof).

Here is one of the twenty times Proverbs mentions laziness: "Work hard and become a leader; be lazy and become a slave" (Proverbs 12:24 NLT).

Paul has some harsh words to say about the matter: "But if any provide not for his own, and specially for those of his own house, he hath denied the faith, and is worse than an infidel" (1 Timothy 5:8).

Don't hold any effort back: "And whatsoever ye do, do it heartily, as to the Lord, and not unto men" (Colossians 3:23).

Laziness leads to many other sorts of struggles which will affect your career, your path, and your life.

Be trustworthy because it not only affects your prosperity on earth but has eternal repercussions. "He that is faithful in that which is least is faithful also in much: and he that is unjust in the least is unjust also in much" (Luke 16:10).

You are representing the Lord. Remember, you are working unto Him and His purpose He has commissioned for your life. Your integrity is on the line, and it will be impossible to lead someone else to Jesus if you are living unrighteously. If you want to live richly, be the most dependable and honorable person on the job.

"He layeth up sound wisdom for the righteous: he is a buckler to them that walk uprightly" (Proverbs 2:7).

Leave no room for stealing, dishonesty, or cheating. Theft has no benefit. "Let him that stole steal no more: **but rather let him labour, working with his hands the thing which is good**, that he may have to give to him that needeth" (Ephesians 4:28). Theft violates others and, therefore, will hurt you and your household in return.

God says that if you lie, cheat, and steal, you are only robbing your own life. "My child, if sinners entice you, turn your back on them! They may say, 'Come and join us. Let's hide and kill someone! Just for fun, let's ambush the innocent! ... Think of the great things we'll get! We'll fill our houses with all the stuff we take. Come, throw in your lot with us; we'll all share the loot' ... But these people set an ambush for themselves; they are trying to get themselves killed. **Such is the fate of all who are greedy for money; it robs them of life**" (Proverbs 1:10-11,13-14,18-19 NLT).

Laziness is encouraged every minute here in the culture of the Western World. So, if you only consume television, social media, non-thought-provoking books, video games, or any other type of mental junk food, don't complain or question your lack of career progress or financial achievement. Instead, begin seeking ways to enhance your knowledge, learn God's ways, make your business dealings intentionally ethical, and build money muscle, moving forward in every way the Lord has directed you to go.

Position In Your Purpose

Yes, you have purpose. God created you to do something that will give Him glory as well as serve others along the way. Yet so many people suffer through life, doing something for which they were not designed to gain money, fame, or other short-sighted outcomes.

If you seek to work in the position that fulfills God's will for your life, you will not only find more joy, peace, and happiness, but meet those temporal needs along the way. Kevin Payne writes:

> *The right thing to do is bring glory to God because there is no one greater who is worthy of trust, adoration, and worship. Therefore, for the Christian, we are to live to bring glory to God— how we do that is through prayer and study of His Word, the Bible, so that we might better know what He has for us.*[5]

Do not hesitate when you hear the voice of the Lord. If you are called, go. There are riches waiting for you at the intersection of God's calling and your obedience. You may not see where this path will ultimately lead, but you will never be disappointed if it is genuinely the Master's plan for your life.

Many times, there are steppingstones, or intermediate positions you must fill today to reach the place God wants you tomorrow. The transition may not be the most glorious, but when you know God has you there for a purpose, it is far more bearable.

Don't forget that while you are working your way towards the ultimate destination, seek not just higher wages, but higher knowledge. I've had positions that were not great pay-wise, but the education was worth more than I would have got through a course in college. During this journey, learning on the job is one of the main purposes overlooked.

As the Lord said to Zerubbabel, **"Do not despise these small beginnings,** for the Lord rejoices to see the work begin"** (Zechariah 4:10a NLT).

It takes hard work, but the rewards are certainly worth it, though not all are monetary. "And we know that all things work together for good to them that love God, to them who are the called according to his purpose" (Romans 8:28).

Patience, as I mentioned in *Biblical Faith Meets Financial Strategy*,[6] plays a huge part. I know too many people who

Many times, there are steppingstones, intermediate positions you must fill today to reach the place God wants you tomorrow.

have rushed into a position that indeed lined up with their purpose, only to find out that it was too soon. They end up moving before it is time, resulting in a missed opportunity where they should have stayed. Or they end up borrowing money to make something happen before its time.

God's timing is not our timing, so you must stay in prayer, faithfully working, listening for His direction, only moving when the time is right. At that divine and perfect moment in your life, a payday will be there waiting for you where your purpose and position intersect.

CHAPTER EIGHT

Learning

You should be a continuous student. If you think you have reached the maximum amount of knowledge you can obtain, your days are indeed numbered. Reading, taking classes, listening to people wiser than you, researching and searching the scriptures for wisdom must continue for you to stay mentally healthy. Your ability to think critically, excel at work, and manage God's resources well is directly correlated with your desire to constantly learn and apply that knowledge. I've seen it time and time again with my own eyes: when learning slows, earning follows.

Gaining knowledge also prevents you from making rash decisions resulting in bad money management. "Enthusiasm without knowledge is no good; haste makes mistakes" (Proverbs 19:2 NLT).

If you stop learning, you may reach the point of mental atrophy. One definition of atrophy is "a gradual decline in effectiveness or vigor due to underuse or neglect."[1] So when you disregard exercising your knowledge of money matters, your financial intellect will slowly decline. Lack of learning about other subjects as well also affects your ability to administer God's wealth.

For example, understanding basic economics may seem boring, but there are many fun ways to grasp these concepts, and this subject can help you invest intelligently. History is more important than most know. If you don't study the past, you are doomed to repeat mistakes that could have been avoided. Also, having a brain stimulating hobby is another example of learning that goes missed. Building, solving, and inventing can exercise those slack brain muscles which later become pivotal levers in business and finance.

The western world has been lulled to sleep by media and entertainment, which I think is one of the reasons for the decline in test scores and measures of intelligence. I will show you some data, but you can see this for yourself in your own city, or even in your own home. If you don't think this affects one's ability to manage money, you are lying to yourself and doing the next generation an injustice.

Bob Yirka with Medical Xpress writes:

> *Prior studies have shown that people grew smarter over the first part of last century, as measured by the intelligence quotient—a trend that was dubbed the Flynn effect … But, now, according to the researchers in Norway, that trend has ended. Instead of getting smarter, humans have started getting dumber.*[2]

This so-called Flynn effect was named after James Flynn who noticed the trend. A 2009 study states:

> *Flynn argues that the abnormal drop in British teenage IQ could be due to youth culture having "stagnated" or even dumbed down. He also states that the youth culture is more oriented towards computer games than towards reading and holding conversations.*[3]

These are not just broad trends but are issues that are blatantly apparent with our knowledge of money. So, let's look at financial IQ in the United States. The National Financial Educators Council created the National Financial Capability Test. "The test measures one's ability to earn, save and grow their finances."[4] At the time of this writing, the average score was 67.9% and 41% of the test takers failed. That's not good.

Corrupt company

leads to

wasted wealth.

We are not teaching finances to our children, most likely because parents don't have the knowledge themselves or don't know how to pass on financial intelligence. Let's change the statistics and begin managing God's Wealth with God's Wisdom. Then let's pass on these money smarts to the next generation.

Here is my formula to increase your financial IQ. It begins with the old school method of learning: reading. Next, we can use technology to increase our financial knowledge (i.e. videos, edutainment, games). Lastly, practice makes perfect; you are going to make mistakes; repetition increase comprehension. So, let's build some money muscle and stay financially fit, beginning with the Book of Proverbs.

Financial Degree from Proverbs

King Solomon is arguably one of the wisest men ever to live. He asked for wisdom, and God blessed him with this gift at a young age. So, if you want some understanding about wealth, turn to his sayings and advice. One of the books of the Bible you can glean from his wisdom is Proverbs.

I have mentioned that there are over 2,000 verses about financial matters in the Bible. Well, quite a few of them are found in Proverbs. There are 31 chapters, so many people have formed the habit of reading "the proverb of the day," meaning the one that corresponds with the day of the month. This would be a wise place for you to begin your financial education. Reading Proverbs daily is like getting a degree in finance. You could ace that financial capability test after studying these 31 chapters.

There is no doubt about the statement with which Proverbs begins. "Their purpose is to teach people to live disciplined and successful lives, to help them do what is right, just, and fair" (Proverbs 1:3 NLT).

So, just to give you a taste of this wisdom, I would like to take you on a journey through this twentieth book of the Bible. The following will be a high-level view of all the financial wisdom contained within. You will see why you should take some time to study these principles, memorize some, and apply them to your everyday life.

- Has someone ever tempted you to join a business opportunity only to find out that it was a scam? Don't fall for it. If it's such a good deal, why do they always need your money instead of investing their own? "My son, if sinners entice thee, consent thou not. If they say ... Cast in thy lot among us; let us all have one purse: My son, walk not thou in the way with them; refrain thy foot from their path ... So are the ways of every one that is greedy of gain; which taketh away the life of the owners thereof" (Proverbs 1:10,14-15,19).

- Everyone wants to live longer to live out their later years, enjoy their grandchildren, travel, and so on. Well, here is the secret to long life. "For length of days, and long life, and peace, shall they add to thee. Let not mercy and truth forsake thee: bind them about thy neck; write them upon the table of thine heart: So shalt thou find favour and good understanding in the sight of God and man" (Proverbs 3:2-4).

- Do you desire to have the problem of figuring out who to bless today? Well, first, you need to have more than enough. And we know from Part II of this book that to have overflowing blessings, you must return the first fruits. "Honour the Lord with thy substance, and with the firstfruits of all thine increase: So shall thy barns be filled with plenty, and thy presses shall burst out with new wine" (Proverbs 3:9-10).

- Help people when you have the means to help them. "Withhold not good from them to whom it is due, when it is in the power of thine hand to do it. Say not unto thy neighbour, Go, and come again, and to morrow I will give; when thou hast it by thee" (Proverbs 3:27-28).

- One of the fastest ways for a man to lose all his wealth is to hang out with immoral women. Ladies, you are not to ignore this advice either. Corrupt company leads to wasted wealth. "Remove thy way far from her, and come not nigh the door of her house: Lest thou give thine honour unto others, and thy years unto the cruel: Lest strangers be filled with thy wealth; and thy labours be in the house of a stranger" (Proverbs 5:8-10).

- Get wisdom, for she holds the keys to real wealth. "Counsel is mine, and sound wisdom: I am understanding; I have strength ... Riches and honour are with me; yea, durable riches and righteousness. My fruit is better than gold, yea, than fine gold; and my revenue than choice silver. I lead in the way of righteousness, in the midst of the paths of judgment: That I may cause those that love me to inherit substance; and I will fill their treasures" (Proverbs 8:14,18-21).

- Wealth gained by cheating becomes a curse. It is always best when you are honest and upright in all your transactions. In the end, the righteous get a lasting reward. "A false balance is abomination to the Lord: but a just weight is his delight … The integrity of the upright shall guide them: but the perverseness of transgressors shall destroy them … The righteousness of the perfect shall direct his way: but the wicked shall fall by his own wickedness. The righteousness of the upright shall deliver them: but transgressors shall be taken in their own naughtiness … The wicked worketh a deceitful work: but to him that soweth righteousness shall be a sure reward" (Proverbs 11:1,3,5-6,18).

- If you want your wealth to grow, it takes planting and investing in the right soil, and since that takes rich fertilizer, it may get a little stinky. "Where no oxen are, the crib is clean: but much

> increase is by the strength of the ox"
> (Proverbs 14:4).

- What has a higher value? Financial riches or a right relationship with God? Keep your priorities straight. "Better is little with the fear of the Lord than great treasure and trouble therewith" (Proverbs 15:16).

And that is just the tip of the iceberg. If you want to go deeper, check out the INTERSECTION Resource Page.[5] I will be regularly updating it with free material to help you learn from this book of wisdom and enable you to pass down this knowledge to future generations. This financial degree is available for everyone.

Higher Education is Overrated

Yes, I said it. Higher education is overrated, meaning, all the credentials people chase to achieve some higher level of employment many times goes to waste. The knowledge needed is many times able to be learned through self-initiated activities and strategies, anyway. The same jobs desired can be obtained with experience and know-how, neither having the prerequisite of a degree.

I didn't say that a bachelors, masters, and doctorate diplomas are a bad thing. I said they are overrated. There is a place for these achievements. But, many times I have found that people can achieve their purpose without the degree they think they need. Of course, there are careers in medicine, law, engineering, and so on, where a higher-level degree is unavoidable. Outside of a select few professions though, you can reach a very well-paying career without a higher education.

Besides this, studies show that 41% of recent graduates get a job where no degree is required, and 73% of college graduates end up working in a field outside of their major.[6] By no means do these statistics imply you should not aim for higher education. But too many people go to university without praying and without a solid plan.

I grew up learning to read technical books about computer application development. Yeah, I know, I was a such a nerd. But it was hugely beneficial as I became extremely proficient at coding, and that skill led me to many jobs and projects that shaped my life.

Today, with the plethora of certifications available with accompanying courses to be used in your free time, there are many paths to follow with no degree required, from surveying, to real estate, to database administration, to hair styling, and beyond. There are many career paths where you can use your skills to earn a large paycheck. Even when the job description calls for a degree, don't let that stop you from pursuing the role if you have the experience. God has a plan for your life right where you are.

Many employers are looking for responsible people who will show up on time and have an eagerness to learn. They can teach someone who is willing to learn, but you will have to display a yearning to do the hard work necessary to excel. On-the-job training is an excellent way to gain the skills needed to get to the level you are aiming for. As an eighteen-year-old, I sought jobs where I could learn and benefit by packing my resume, so that later I could apply for those highly sought after positions backed up by several recommendations and months or years of experience. That beats the competition with their four-year degree and nothing but outdated book smarts every time.

You can enhance that experience on your own time as well. The most beneficial resource many people have at their fingertips is reading. When I recommend a book, I'm still shocked every time someone says, "I don't read." And then I remembered I was the same way. Until I was in my twenties, I had not read a non- computer programming book. I know that's crazy. I thought I was an oddball, but I found that this is, unfortunately, the case with many people.

Today, I love reading non-fiction because God has developed in me a ferocious appetite for learning something new. Plus, since it takes multiple times to understand anything before I get it, reading a variety of books on the same subject happens often. Being a slow reader, I find it helps me to listen to an audiobook, while reading along with the physical book, highlighter in hand. So, if you are not a fast reader either, maybe that tip can help you overcome this obstacle.

Over time, I now realize that this was the perfect complement to my desire to manage God's Wealth with God's Wisdom. It turns out there are tons of outstanding books about the many facets of finance with Godly inspiration. (And I pray this one becomes one of them.)

Reading is pivotal. It is a crucially important habit you must develop if you want to manage money in your life efficiently. There are financial, business, and economics books for all ages and stages of life. You can start by reading to your children or grandchildren. Believe me, you may learn just as much as they do.

You must begin by strengthening that reading muscle. If you don't have a habit of reading, the first book is painful. But if you read consistently, it gets more comfortable; you get faster, and it becomes habitual. It's just like physical exercise.

Speaking of physical exercise, you can pair these two healthy habits together. Try walking, running, or cycling while listening to an audiobook about personal finances. Your budget will drop pounds right along with your body!

Also, you don't have to read financial education books only. As I mentioned, there are many subjects that can help you solve problems and think smarter. This will help you become more successful. When you read books that exercise your brain, you positively affect your entire life. Here are the key benefits of reading, according to Healthline:[7]

- *improves brain connectivity*
- *increases your vocabulary and comprehension*
- *empowers you to empathize with other people*
- *aids in sleep readiness*
- *reduces stress*
- *lowers blood pressure and heart rate*
- *fights depression symptoms*
- *prevents cognitive decline as you age*
- *contributes to a longer life*

And guess what? When you realize some of these benefits, you make more money. Employers like to hire people with vast competencies, from troubleshooting to analytical skills. You may start your own business with all your newfound wisdom. Promotions will come your way because if it is between you and someone who has the same time on the job, you have the edge.

By the way, since you are earning money earlier than someone who is in school, you can save a portion for a degree later in life. Plus, many employers will have tuition reimbursement, making that degree free. The point is not to dismiss higher-level education completely, but to think about its necessity at the right time.

One last point on reading. It has benefits far and wide, but there is one book you must read every day because it has exceedingly significant advantages: the Holy Bible, the number one bestseller of all time. You know the Bible has many verses that will help you grow spiritually and financially, but did you know you learn other subjects too? Everything from history to mathematics to science and beyond. Believe me; it's all in there. Maybe, the government taking the Bible out of schools has aided in the decline of those IQ scores. Just a thought.

Theodore Roosevelt once said, "A thorough knowledge of the Bible is worth more than a college education." And, as the Bible itself teaches, "All Scripture is God-breathed and is **useful for teaching**, rebuking, correcting and training in righteousness" (2 Timothy 3:16 NIV).

But, you may have experienced a university professor that says the Bible is nothing but fairy tales and God is dead. Have you ever heard of a scholarly fool?

Where Wisdom Meets Real Education

Don't rely on government schools alone. Teach your children, nieces, nephews, godchildren, neighbors' kids wisdom at the kitchen table. We don't talk about money at the home, but we should.

I grew up observing what I could about managing money and juggling the check register. I had no teacher; therefore, I learned little. The many mistakes that ensued were of course great instructors, but learning at the school of hard knocks is not the best way by a long shot.

Leaving an inheritance doesn't begin after you die. It starts on the couch, during bedtime stories, and on the back porch. You need to start by leaving an inheritance of wisdom from the Word of God, or they will waste the wealth you pass on. You must train the one to whom you are passing the torch.

"A good man leaveth an inheritance to his children's children: and the wealth of the sinner is laid up for the just" (Proverbs 13:22).

I believe many of the households today don't teach their children about money matters because of a combination of these three reasons:

1. They don't know how to handle finances themselves. So, they don't know what to teach. They are still making terrible mistakes with money, so they hide their shortcomings and just don't talk about them.

2. Mom and Dad are uncomfortable talking about wealth. They don't want the kids to know because it embarrasses them to reveal how they handle their Inflow and Outgo. Also, they have this idea that it is none of their children's business. "This is an adult matter, after all," they say. Yet they openly discuss politics, for example, which is far less significant.

3. They are too busy and don't feel it is necessary to take the time to discuss

this critical topic. Any of these situations could involve a single parent, but especially this situation. You are doing the best that you can, so you think. Making sure they brush their teeth and do their homework is all the energy you can muster. Taking five minutes to impart some of the most important knowledge they will have obtained throughout their day doesn't even cross your mind.

But by not talking about it, you are setting up your children for failure.

I think parents often find it easier to talk about sex and religion than about prosperity. You know about sex, and everyone has to have "the talk." And religion is a generational thing: "We go to church because that's what we do," we exclaim.

So, since we are so vocal about these other pivotal topics, why not money too? Well, I declare that this silence must stop now. You are the solution. You must decide to begin a new trend now, at least in your family line.

"Direct your children onto the right path, and when they are older, they will not leave it" (Proverbs 22:6 NLT).

You must talk about these matters freely with your children and encourage them to do the same. If your adult children don't want to pass on the torch, you must share this information with your grandchildren as well. Declare: silence surrounding money ends now.

Not only teach them, but remind them, and even write letters to them, as King Solomon did:

> *My son, if thou wilt receive my words, and hide my commandments with thee; So that thou incline thine ear unto wisdom, and apply thine heart to understanding; Yea, if thou criest after knowledge, and liftest up thy voice for understanding; If thou seekest her as silver, and searchest for her as for hid treasures; Then shalt thou understand the fear of the Lord, and find the knowledge of God. For the Lord giveth wisdom: out of his mouth cometh knowledge and understanding (Proverbs 2:1-6).*

Don't forget to use technology to keep them (and you) engaged. Admittedly, the Internet has a lot of trash, but there is a lot of expert knowledge there, too. As a wise man once told me, "Eat the meat and spit out the bones."

Search YouTube for videos that align with your values and have the wisdom that you are looking for. Instead of the news, which is the worst way to end your evening (in my opinion), I would turn on the Dave Ramsey Show to listen with the family at dinnertime. We would laugh, comment, and learn some financial wisdom together.

There are board games, video games, and even quizzes and online mini courses that you can use to learn more and pass on money intellect. I will keep a growing list on the INTERSECTION Resource Page[5], so check it out for ideas that you can apply to your life.

As I mentioned at the beginning of this chapter, practice makes perfect. This is how good managers become brilliant managers. Once again, it's about combating our natural laziness and stopping excuse making. By not seeking more knowledge on your own, you miss out on your calling; you are at the mercy of what society at large preaches; you earn far less than your potential. Work hard; become wealthy in resources and wisdom, and then pass on that knowledge and insight to the next generation.

In the next chapter, I'll dive into how to put all this knowledge into action by managing well, but don't forget to continuously stay educated and keep passing it down. This is a lifelong journey and will forever shape your legacy.

CHAPTER NINE

Managing

I've learned that you must intentionally obey and respect your parents, your boss at work, and all other forms of authority. It is natural to question everything and desire to do things your way. The same goes even more so for being a good steward and faithful manager of God's resources.

As I mentioned in *Biblical Faith Meets Financial Strategy*,[1] Chapter 2, prayer is where real financial success is rooted. Let me add, as you thank God for all His provisions and ask for the things that are on your heart and mind, obedience must follow. Abide by His Word as He speaks to you.

Think about when a child asks her parent for something. Many times, the parent responds, "Do this first." Now the child has a choice. She can obey, or she can disobey. Assuming the parent is not asking the child to do something evil, we know that disobedience is not the right choice. But compliance can be wrong as well when done with a negative mindset. Obedience with the wrong attitude is not honorable.

"Sometimes children obey but they do it with a bad attitude. Honor is the solution. It's important to teach children what honor means in very practical terms ... Obedience is revealed in actions. Honor is revealed in the attitude that goes along with those actions."[2]

When you read the Bible, let the words speak to you and your current situation. And when you pray, praise for sure, ask—if you feel led—but don't forget to be quiet and listen. The voice of the Lord will be clear and, many times, convicting. His answer always aligns with His Word, and we as managers always manage according to the Owner's instructions.

You have a loving Father in Heaven that wants to give you your heart's desire. But you must be willing to obey His will for your life. Have you ever read the Lord's prayer? Reread it, but this time through the lenses of one who manages with honor, obedience, and submission.

"After this manner therefore pray ye: Our Father which art in heaven, Hallowed be thy name. Thy kingdom come. Thy will be done in earth, as it is in heaven. Give us this day our daily bread. And forgive us our debts, as we forgive our debtors. And lead us not into temptation, but deliver us from evil: For thine is the kingdom, and the power, and the glory, for ever. Amen" (Matthew 6:9-13).

Test every thought you have in prayer with scripture, for the Bible never fails. You will find many answers to questions you have, and you can trust the solutions you receive. His daily bread will give you the physical energy, spiritual strength, and the proper money mindset to succeed.

Now it is up to you to be obedient and do so with a cheerful disposition. Your attitude matters, and it is most honorable to obey with a grateful heart. Now that you are working and learning according to faith, it's time to apply some strategy to the deep desire to manage well.

Manage the Garden

God commanded Adam to tend to and keep the garden, and so it is your job, too. I know I am repeating myself, but the budget is the primary tool to be a good financial steward. Don't cringe; it isn't so bad. A prayerful plan is there for your accountability. To budget is to use Godly Wisdom as you manage God's Wealth.

To budget, you need a personal accounting system. There are several methods to accomplish this. I am a big fan of using pencil and paper, keeping the books the old-fashioned way. You could take advantage of the power of a spreadsheet program. There are free apps you could use, and there are even more robust computer applications made for the task. It doesn't matter which one you choose. Just pick something you can grasp and will not prevent you from staying consistent.

If you are married, you must keep track of and plan your resources together. This is crucially important. Many couples unknowingly create an atmosphere of stress and worry in their marriage by keeping individual checking accounts, for example. When you spoke those vows, you should have known that you were pledging to become one. This includes all money matters.

Not only should you combine all bank accounts, but your planning, budgeting, dreaming, and legacy planning should be together as well. When done individually, it becomes more complicated to see the complete picture. It's not *my* accounting and *their* accounting, it is *our* accounting. So, every transaction affects the entire money management system for the household.

Adam and Eve were to manage the wealth of the garden together. If you notice, God told Adam to not touch His portion before creating Eve. So, it was Adam's job to communicate the principle of the first fruits or the tree set apart, to Eve. Also, notice that Satan came to tempt Eve to eat and take what was not hers to touch, not Adam. Where was Adam? Did Adam tell Eve exactly what God had told him? We don't get all the details, but something did go wrong.

The lack of communication is one of the top reasons for marriages splitting up in America. Money problems are another prime cause for the rise in divorce. I bet that miscommunication about money tops the list. This is an intersection you never want to aim for. That's because when you are married, money management is a team sport. God expects you to abide by the laws of the garden together.

So, promise me you will never just hand over the responsibility to your spouse because you don't want to be involved (all in the name of "trust"). That is not trust; that is being willfully ignorant. And promise that you stop the lie of "his money" and "her money." It is neither of your money. It's all God's, and it is both of your responsibility to manage it well.

Romans 14:12 states, "So then every one of us shall give account of himself to God." I believe this is speaking about your life holistically, including finances. There is more to life than money, so you must be accountable as a parent, a spouse, a minister, a neighbor, an employee, and a friend. But your heart and your treasure are in the same place. How you handle finances says a lot about your character.

We should look at how we are doing and where we are going as we manage His resources. It is healthy to be aware of your faithfulness. So, I created a resource to help you along on this journey of managing God's wealth with excellence. Download the *God's Ownership Meets Money*

If you are married, not only should you combine all bank accounts, but your planning, budgeting, dreaming, and legacy planning should be together as well.

Management SWOT Analysis worksheet on the resource page: **intersection.zeroinfinancial.com**.

Jesus uses money in a parable when describing the good and faithful servant. You must account for the resources you are managing and, therefore, show your faithfulness. The reward for stewarding well is riches we can't even comprehend. The prize is real wealth, not like the currency we have here on earth.

I will go deeper into this parable in a moment, but I want to point out the words the Master had for the steward who managed well: "His lord said unto him, Well done, thou good and faithful servant: thou hast been faithful over a few things, I will make thee ruler over many things: enter thou into the joy of thy lord" (Matthew 25:21).

Just by managing God's Wealth with God's Wisdom, you can expect to enter the joy of the Lord.

The Matthew Henry Commentary explains, "This joy is the joy of their Lord; the joy which he himself has purchased and provided for them; the joy of the redeemed, bought with the sorrow of the Redeemer. It is the joy which he himself is in the possession of, and which he had his eye upon when he endured the cross, and despised the shame."[3]

Jesus purchased this joy with His blood. And this is the reward for being faithful and managing well. I'm sure once we get to enter into this place, we will forget all about those earthly resources.

Investing What You Manage

In Matthew 25, Jesus uses parables to describe the kingdom of heaven. In each of these stories, He uses money and possessions to make His point. We can all relate to these examples because we live in a world with material goods where we reap what we sow. Therefore, these parables are not only critical in understanding heaven and the return of Christ, but they are also useful in learning how to have a Godly mindset with money.

The first parable is about ten virgins going to meet the bridegroom. Of course, Jesus is the bridegroom of the church, which is His bride. This story is all about being ready. In it, five of the virgins are wise and the other five are foolish. But what do half of them do that the other half do not? They keep a reserve.

The first and most important way to invest what you earn is by saving a portion. I wrote about the need for an emergency fund in *Biblical Faith Meets Financial Strategy*, but it is also essential to save for future large expenditures.

For example, sinking funds are accounts in which you save money to replace or buy things in the future. You may know you have to replace your roof in three years, so you save a small amount each month for thirty-six months, building up enough to pay for the planned expense in cash. You can do the same for a car, your washing machine, and any other sizeable future expenditure.

You can use reserve savings for everything, from entertainment to charity. I cover strategic giving in *Divine Provision Meets Generosity Planning*, so let's take vacations, for an example. My family has an Excursion Fund, where we save up a few hundred dollars every month. When we want to go on vacation or find out about a travel deal, we have the money set aside to take that holiday with no worries, without borrowing a penny, and with no regrets.

"The wise have wealth and luxury, but fools spend whatever they get" (Proverbs 21:20 NLT).

In the second parable in Matthew 25, Jesus describes three managers. Their master left them each an amount of money described as a talent, proportionate to their ability. One received a talent, another received two talents, and the third steward received five talents.

As a side note, there are people today who believe everyone should receive an equal portion, touted as "equity." They say, "It is not fair for one person to receive more than another." But this mindset does not align with the Bible. God blesses each of us as He sees fit and as our capacity to manage dictates. God does not give us more than we can handle, nor does He give us less than we ought to have.

Our job as a good steward is to invest well with what we have in our possession to manage. The parable ends with the master returning to receive an account of their investment strategies. The stewards of two and five talents have doubled the money, and the master replies, "Well done, good and faithful servant." But this was not the case for the last servant.

> *Then he which had received the one talent came and said, Lord, I knew thee that thou art an hard man, reaping where thou hast not sown, and gathering where thou hast not strawed: And I was afraid, and went and hid thy talent in the earth: lo, there thou hast that is thine. His lord answered and said unto him, Thou wicked and slothful servant, thou knewest that I reap where I sowed not, and gather where I have not strawed: Thou oughtest therefore to have put my money to the exchangers, and then at my coming I should have received mine own with usury (Matthew 25:24-27).*

Investing needs to be a part of a healthy financial plan. As the master pointed out, the last servant could have at least put the money into a savings account to gain some interest. Doing nothing with money is not a righteous plan.

After budgeting and praying about the proper amount needed for living expenses, planning a portion to save in emergency and reserve accounts, and giving according to the prompting of the Holy Spirit, you must invest.

There are many resources that can assist you in this area. And not understanding investing is not an excuse to stay uneducated about investment matters. We are to grow the Master's Wealth with the Master's Wisdom.

"Send your grain across the seas, and in time, profits will flow back to you. But divide your investments among many places, for you do not know what risks might lie ahead" (Ecclesiastes 11:1-2 NLT).

Entrepreneurship is Biblical

I must add a small section here about being an entrepreneur. Starting a venture is not the path for every person. But as our kids grow up, we rarely mention this option as they wonder, "What am I going to be when I grow up?" This career path seems to be the red-headed stepchild of potential positions.

Also, when we think of investing, we think about securities, commodities, real estate, and so on, but we must not forget about investing in business. It seems scary for many people, but it just requires a dedication to education and hard work. Anything can seem scary when you don't understand it, or it is new. The first step is to learn; then one can be inspired to test the waters.

I will not go in depth into how to begin a business, but I want to encourage you to leave this as an option. There will be resources on intersection.zeroinfinancial.com[4] for you to do a deeper dive.

Your purpose may mean being a solopreneur or even a future employer. What a great privilege—to provide

Never say you can't

be a missionary and

create an income.

income to families, employment opportunities to your community, and products or services to the world. You may even be led to develop a non-profit or for-profit social venture, solving one of the many critical global issues we daily face.

And, I have great news; being an entrepreneur is Biblical! Here are three of the Bible's world-renowned businesspeople:

1. Abraham, the father of our faith, was a successful businessman in the cattle industry. He had many employees to manage his vast growing herd. Because of Abraham's understanding of who owns it all and where blessing originates, God continued to make him prosperous. Having a legacy mindset, he could pass on the business as generational wealth.

    The Lord appeared to his son Isaac while in Egypt and told him He would bless him just like his dad. God explained why He would bless him and why He blessed Abraham in business: "Because that Abraham obeyed my voice, and kept my charge, my commandments, my statutes, and my laws" (Genesis 26:5). Obedience to the

Provider of all results in business success.

2. The woman of Proverbs 31 may be the perfect model entrepreneur. She works with her hands, making products with wool, flax, and fine linen, marketing all her goods worldwide. It mentions her investing in property where she grows a vineyard. She seems to be a serial entrepreneur; I can relate.

   Two interesting facts about this woman of God are her work ethic and her dependence on God's wisdom. "She makes sure her dealings are profitable; her lamp burns late into the night" (Proverbs 31:18 NLT). So, she works extremely hard and knows the importance of turning a profit. She is virtuous and speaks words of wisdom and kindness.

   Oh, by the way, she is a faithful wife and mother. So never say you must choose between being a talented businesswoman and having a family. If God has chosen you for this purpose, you can have both through His wisdom and guidance.

3. And then let's not forget the Apostle
    Paul. We know him as the one who
    wrote two-thirds of the New
    Testament according to the inspiration
    of the Holy Spirit. But while
    proclaiming the Gospel of Jesus
    Christ, he also earned a living. He was
    a small business owner of a tent
    company, including manufacturing and
    selling.

    This business allowed Paul to be
    self-supporting during his ministry. We
    also see how he supported himself and
    the missionary team and was generous
    in helping others too. "Yea, ye
    yourselves know, that these hands have
    ministered unto my necessities, and to
    them that were with me. I have shewed
    you all things, how that so labouring ye
    ought to support the weak, and to
    remember the words of the Lord Jesus,
    how he said, It is more blessed to give
    than to receive" (Acts 20:34-35).

    The occupation also benefited him
    by providing lodging as he traveled, for
    he stayed with other tentmakers;
    having this commonality opened up
    opportunity. Paul even used his work

ethic as a teaching point as he writes to the church in Thessalonica, "For even when we were with you, this we commanded you, that if any would not work, neither should he eat" (2 Thessalonians 3:10).

You can discover much more about acts of generosity in *Divine Provision Meets Generosity Planning*.[5]

Never say you can't be a missionary and create an income. Through God, all things are possible. And if it is His will for your life, who can stop you from doing both? He may even make a way for you to serve in a particular country. Your business could open that door that is typically closed.

What great examples of Christians who used the talent God gave them to create ventures for the Lord. So, no matter what your purpose is and what God has called you to do, don't rule out starting a business. Though you may go into business for yourself, you will never be by yourself; God will be there with you all the way.

There should be no shame in being successful. Unfortunately, I must mention this toxic idea. Some believe it is evil to create lots of profit or to accumulate great wealth. Others even think it is ungodly when a Christian is not living super lean or even poor. This is neither Biblical nor the will of God.

God calls us all for His purpose, but individually. Some He may use in a way where that person owns extraordinarily little and can do great things in the poorest nations of the world with no enormous church or organization behind them. Money for them is of no concern, but even they understand that resources for the people they serve need to come from somewhere.

That is where God used great businesswomen and businessmen who have a heart for the mission field. They provide the needed resources through donations, through skilled laborers, and through knowledge of how to solve the most complicated issues.

Glory be to God for mission-driven entrepreneurs! Thank God for those who have no shame in being successful! Praise God for the richest brothers and sisters who know that none of the money they have is theirs, and they are working to become the best managers of God's wealth! You could be one of these; but remember, it starts by providing for your home and grows from there.

I have always dreamed of helping people in this area, and many don't know where to turn to get started. This is one reason financial coaching is so powerful. I not only help employees, I walk alongside entrepreneurs as they grow their business for God's glory. If you want to know more, please schedule a call, and then we can continue the conversation in a special complimentary consultation for prospective entrepreneurs. Reach out via the contact page on zeroinfinancial.com. Believe me, being in business is a blast!

CHAPTER TEN

Money Management by The Ten Commandments

The late Zig Ziglar once said, "If God would have wanted us to live in a permissive society He would have given us Ten Suggestions and not Ten Commandments."

The Ten Commandments received by Moses on Mount Sinai are remarkably simple and super relevant. They are as applicable today as they were when God wrote them with His finger on stone tablets. They are even reinforced in the New Testament as you will see.

Dennis Prager, author of *The Rational Bible* series, (which contains his commentary of Exodus titled *The Rational Bible: Exodus*), taught the first five books of the

Hebrew Bible (the Torah) for more than twenty-five years at the American Jewish University in Los Angeles. Dennis is also author of *The Ten Commandments: Still the Best Moral Code,*[1] where he describes it as "all that is necessary to make a good world."

Unfortunately, these commandments from God have been removed from court houses, schools, and all other types of government institutions all around the world. This list of momentous instructions are no longer spoken about or taught at home to children as guidelines for living a wholesome life. We have seen no good effect on society due to this subtle transition away from its foundational message from God.

Let's dive into Exodus Chapter 20 and see how these laws not only guide you to be a good person but can help you manage money as God intends for you. I will also show you how the New Testament mirrors and enhances each commandment. So, let's look at Money Management by the Ten Commandments.

THOU SHALT HAVE NO OTHER GODS BEFORE ME

[Exodus 20:3] You cannot serve two masters; but many Americans are slave to the lender. As Dave Ramsey says, "Why do you think they named it MasterCard?" There is a dangerous false god named Mammon, "often used to describe the debasing influence of material wealth ...

Medieval writers commonly interpreted it as an evil demon or god."[2]

We slowly fade away from putting God first in every area of our lives, including money, to allowing the world to put many other gods before our eyes. And so we seek more work, more pay, more overtime, more advancement up the ladder, with no concern if this is the path the Master desires. We replace reading the Bible with binge-watching television and endlessly scrolling on our devices. We replace going to church with mindless prosperity-destroying activities and hobbies.

Reinforced under the New Covenant: "...ye should turn from these vanities unto the living God, which made heaven, and earth, and the sea, and all things that are therein" (Acts 14:15).

Only serve the Creator and Owner of Everything, Inc. Faith in anyone and anything else is faith in a false god and founded on a shaky foundation. Vanity and materialism are the worship of money and the stuff money buys. So obeying this commandment is to turn from the world's way of managing resources and towards God's way of managing His resource for His glory.

I mentioned in *Biblical Faith Meets Financial Strategy* that you need to check your financial pulse. In Chapter 7, I mentioned that loaded verse Luke 17:32: "Remember Lot's wife." This verse is a warning to those who have allowed the desires and things of this world to replace God as Lord of your life. Don't allow other gods to be before the God of gods as Lot's wife did.

Active Christianity says it best:

> *Many people ... admire or worship all kinds of created things—like intelligence, beauty, influence, wealth, accomplishments, and talent—instead of honoring or worshiping God. Consequently they are prone to things like idolizing people, jealousy, sexual immorality, covetousness, pride, unthankfulness, being bound by what people think of them and much, much more. If we were to see higher than all these created things to the Creator of all things, we would see that the only value and meaning in all of these things is such as can be used for God's glory!* [3]

THOU SHALT NOT MAKE UNTO THEE ANY GRAVEN IMAGE

[Exodus 20:4] Today, people worship possessions from automobiles, to houses, to jewelry, and beyond. But, maybe even more so, today's graven images appear on our smartphones and the Internet, thanks to social media and unlimited video content.

So many times, we find throughout the Bible, God's people turning towards the worship of idols which represented wealth and prosperity, Baal being the chief one. This would always end in misery and destruction of the very thing to which they paid homage.

As you read through the Old Testament, you will find worshiping the graven image of Baal was at the center of the many Israelite backslidings.

> *Baal (ba'al) was an ancient Canaanite and Mesopotamian deity associated with agriculture. He was believed to be the "giver of life" and mankind was dependent upon him for providing what was necessary to sustain the farms, flocks and herds. He was also called the "son of Dagon" (who was in control of the grain), and "Hadad" the storm god who would provide plentiful rains after hearing his voice (thunder).*[4]

As you can see, the children of Isreal turned away from the Maker of Heaven and Earth, and the One who provides life, sustenance, and provision, to a false god who was praised as the source. We do the same today, sometimes with physical graven images, sometimes virtual.

Reinforced under the New Covenant: "Forasmuch then as we are the offspring of God, we ought not to think that the Godhead is like unto gold, or silver, or stone, graven by art and man's device" (Acts 17:29).

God is not a lucky charm and doesn't live in idols or images. People put their faith in everything from crucifixes to rosary beads, to stock ticker symbols, to horoscopes, to fortune cookies ... instead of faith in the One who lives in and through our lives. People say they were "lucky" when God provides a blessing. They wish and hope for success instead of honestly praying and knowing that the Almighty is in control.

Only manage money by the guidance of the Holy Spirit, who directs us through every decision and situation. Thank God for everything He provides, both big and small. It's okay to have stuff; just never allow that stuff to have you.

There are substances that are mined from the earth that are so called "precious," both metals and rocks: gold, silver, diamonds, etc. Likewise, we give great value to real estate, cryptocurrency, luxury vehicles, unique coins, comic books, and so many other objects. Please invest in wherever God leads you, to save and multiply money, but these commodities and rare earth metals and stones are not really precious when you look at them through a Biblical lens. These are all common day graven images people worship.

When you realize that Jesus and His salvation is the only thing truly precious in life, anxiety about those investments goes away. This perspective is critical because markets rise and fall, but Jesus is our immovable cornerstone. I've seen people go into depression and consider suicide over lost investments. This doesn't happen when your life is rooted in faith beyond this world's financial idols.

THOU SHALT NOT TAKE
THE NAME OF THE LORD THY GOD IN VAIN

[**Exodus 20:7**] Have you ever seen fellow employees making rude comments about the owner behind their back? Or maybe you've done this yourself. This is a very unhealthy practice, but it's far worse when that Owner is God. Never use His name as a swear word or with disrespect.

If a child lies to her dad, stomps her feet, whines, complains, and uses her dad's name in vain having no respect, how eagerly will he be to give whatever she then asks for later that day? God does not think or act like us humans; but we are made in His image. We should reverence the Lord, not just to get what we want when we pray, but because He deserves all the honor and praise. When referring to the Lord, let it be sincere and with admiration.

This is another place where you can clearly see the intersection of God's Wealth and God's Wisdom. "He has paid a full ransom for his people. He has guaranteed his covenant with them forever. What a holy, awe-inspiring name he has! Fear of the Lord is the foundation of true wisdom. All who obey his commandments will grow in wisdom. Praise him forever!" (Psalm 111:9-10 NLT)

As you can see here, God has redeemed us with a guarantee. With great respect, we should glorify his "awe-inspiring name."

Another phrase for reverencing God is "the Fear of the Lord," and this is indeed the beginning of all wisdom. Charles Bridges in describing the Fear of the Lord writes, "It is that affectionate reverence by which the child of God bends himself humbly and carefully to his Father's law."[5] You need this wisdom to manage His wealth.

Reinforced under the New Covenant: Jesus gave a template for how a good steward prays: "After this manner therefore pray ye: Our Father which art in heaven, Hallowed be thy name" (Matthew 6:9).

The name of the Lord is worthy to be praised. Work while respecting the Owner's name. Manage while reverencing the Owner just the same.

Here are just a few of the names of our God. Use them when praying to Him depending on your needs. He loves when we use His name respectfully and will faithfully respond.

- El Chuwl: The God Who Gave You Birth
- El Shaddai: God Almighty
- El Deah: The God of Knowledge
- Elohim: The Creator
- Jehovah-Rapha: The Lord Who Heals You
- Jehovah-Jireh: The LORD Our Provider
- Jehovah-Shalom: The LORD is Peace

In every area of life, especially in managing all resources, you can boldly call on His name. How could you ever use His name is vain when he is …

- The Helper
- Maker of all things
- The Vine
- Your Inheritance
- The Bread of Life
- Your Exceeding Great Reward
- The One Who Comforts You

I recommend you do a study on the many names of God. You, your family, and your plan will be blessed.

REMEMBER THE SABBATH DAY, TO KEEP IT HOLY

[**Exodus 20:8**] God rested on the seventh day as an example to us. He didn't need to rest, but as the Great Leader, He showed how His workers should go about their business. Since He created us, He knows what our bodies and minds need in order to operate at peak performance. We need renewal, and that is what the sabbath is all about.

The sabbath is not only about physical rest but is as much about worship. We can get so busy that we need a weekly reminder to set aside time to thank and praise the Provider of all. Also, we may find that this day set aside can give us new focus for the other six days.

When studying the Jewish sabbath traditions and way of life, I noticed many people are concerned with what they may not do. I was more curious to know what they did on this Holy day. Here are a few of what many modern

Jews do on Shabbat, that is, from sundown Friday to sundown Saturday:

- Praying at home
- Eating with friends and family
- Taking walks together
- Going to bed early
- Attending synagogue to learn and pray
- Singing around the table
- Reading
- Taking a nap
- Playing sports and board games

Reinforced under the New Covenant: Jesus said that He is Lord of the sabbath (Matthew 12:8, Mark 2:28, Luke 6:5). Then he exclaims: "Come unto me, all ye that labour and are heavy laden, and I will give you rest" (Matthew 11:28).

As I revealed in Chapter 7, proper rest yields to greater efficiency, which of course results in managing God's wealth well. Today we work ourselves at an inefficient pace.

> Then Jesus said to them, "The Sabbath was made to meet the needs of people, and not people to meet the requirements of the Sabbath" (Mark 2:27 NLT).

If we took that one day to pray, spend time with family, nap, sing, read the bible, and enjoy our leisure, how much more energized would we be at work throughout the week!

God's laws and commandments are like vitamins for success and productivity. If you want to enhance your financial health, keep this commandment.

HONOUR THY FATHER AND THY MOTHER

[**Exodus 20:12**] To honor authority means to intentionally and joyfully obey. Honor is defined as high respect and great esteem. And the reward for obeying is very significant.

As seen with the second commandment, reverence goes a long way. God gave us these laws not to control His people but to teach us theses important truths. Respecting your pastor, boss, police, teachers, and all others in authority results in more success and open doors. But parents hold an even higher place of honor (of course, assuming a non-abusive situation).

Above all, you should honor God, our Father and the parent of all life, and this should continue from generation to generation. He knows that this relationship is where wisdom is passed down and great lessons of life are learned. Real generational wealth happens where wise parents intersect with respectful children. Now that's what I call a healthy home.

Reinforced under the New Covenant: "Honour thy father and mother; which is the first commandment with promise" (Ephesians 6:2).

Real generational

wealth happens

where wise parents

intersect with

respectful children.

And this commandment comes with a promise of blessing. Ephesians continues, "… that it may be well with thee, and thou mayest live long on the earth" (verse 3). Another dollar does us no good if we are not alive to enjoy the fruits of our labor.

Long life is a glorious reward indeed. Amongst the greatest desires of someone on their deathbed, more time tops the list. And if you look at Exodus 20:12 closely, you see that the promise of a long life is so that you can enjoy the wealth God has given you.

THOU SHALT NOT KILL

[Exodus 20:13] The punishment God assigned Cain, the first murderer, shows how this sin affects resources and prosperity. "When thou tillest the ground, it shall not henceforth yield unto thee her strength; a fugitive and a vagabond shalt thou be in the earth." (Genesis 4:12)

The sixth through eight commandments are the shortest of the ten. They're concise and to the point. No further explanation is necessary because people can immediately see the repercussions. In the history of modern governments, this is one of the few crimes for which capital punishment has been legalized.

And even worse …

Reinforced under the New Covenant: "But the fearful, and unbelieving, and the abominable, and **murderers**, and whoremongers, and sorcerers, and idolaters, and all liars, shall have their part in the lake which burneth with fire and brimstone: which is the second death" (Revelation 21:8).

Here you see that hell is the ultimate penalty for murder, along with idolaters (2nd commandment), adulterers (7th commandment), and liars (9th commandment). This is serious! Praise God He sent His one and only Son to redeem anyone who accepts His salvation.

Most people say, "I'm a good person. I haven't murdered anyone." But Jesus says that hating someone is the same as murder (Matthew 5:22), and murder comes with the above very stern warning from Revelation. Just as honor produces long life, hatred results in a bitter end. And as we see from Cain's penalty, all your success and prosperity will come to nothing if anger and wrath consume you.

This commandment is the antidote to cancel culture. People who hold grudges and treat others without love rarely thrive in life. It's as if the more you hold back, the less you have. Hating others leads to misery; Loving others leads to liberty.

THOU SHALT NOT COMMIT ADULTERY

[Exodus 20:14] Adultery results from unchecked lust. Its characteristics include infidelity and cheating. Writing Explained states: "The proverb 'Cheaters never prosper' simply means that those who gain an advantage at something by cheating will ultimately have to face the consequences of their actions."[6] Adulterers have momentary pleasure with no thought of the pending outcome.

Also, God uses this truth of adultery when describing His people as being unfaithful to Him. This goes back to the first commandment of having no other god before Him. The church is the bride of Christ, and when we disobey and disrespect, we are being unfaithful and commit adultery.

Just like the understanding of a child honoring his parents leads to a fruitful life, the blessings of a faithful husband or wife are abundant.

Reinforced under the New Covenant: "Marriage is honourable in all, and the bed undefiled: but whoremongers and adulterers God will judge" (Hebrews 13:4).

Marriages have enough challenges without adding a lack of communication about money. Rachel Cruze coined the term "financial infidelity" in describing the act of lying to your spouse about money, hiding financial transactions, and breaking the contract (or budget) you both agreed to keep.[7] Do not commit financial adultery; the consequence is not something you want.

I must tell this story because when it happened, I didn't know whether to laugh or cry. I did both. While recently working at the local gas station, I had a customer come in and bring a bottle of alcohol to the counter.

Then he whipped out his credit card and said, "I'm want to charge $20, so put the difference on pump #2."

I replied with a confused, "Okay."

He was happy to explain, "When the old lady asks, it was all for filling up the gas tank. My dad taught me how to do it like this. We call it WOOL money."

"What is WOOL money?" I asked.

He smiled, "Woman Out Of the Loop money."

There it was! Financial infidelity right before my eyes!

Marriage is to be honorable in "all," and that includes finances. Couples agree to a lifelong covenant, and when one or both parties lack integrity with money, the contract has been injured. This is a subtle sin and financial infidelity, as well as adultery rarely happens overnight. Watch out for the signs in your marriage, and repent and turn around before it becomes a bigger problem.

THOU SHALT NOT STEAL

[Exodus 20:15] From the beginning of time, we see that taking or using resources or money that does not belong to you comes with a curse. In the same way, when you don't tithe, you are in fact stealing the Lord's portion. When you return the tithe, you are being obedient, which comes with a blessing.

In the Roman Empire, thieves were convicted like murderers. When Christ was crucified, there were two thieves crucified on either side of Him. One thief repented in his last moments of life and was assured of eternal life in heaven. It's never too late to turn to Jesus!

There are a host of ways we violate this commandment today. Be careful not to miss the ways we can be financially unethical with God's wealth, like taking home something from the office not allowed to be removed. Not all stealing is robbery, shoplifting, burglary, or petty theft. Stealing includes dishonest business dealings as well.

Cheating on your taxes is theft and is never acceptable. Cheating includes under the table money and not reporting tips, because you are lying on the tax form when it asked if you received any unreported income. You may think that you are saving money or making your income stretch further, but don't miss what Jesus said: "Render unto Caesar what is Caesar's."

Reinforced under the New Covenant: "Let him that stole steal no more: but rather let him labour, working with his hands the thing which is good, that he may have to give to him that needeth" (Ephesians 4:28).

In this New Testament verse, we see we should not only resist theft, we should also give. We honestly work, learn, manage, and earn, so that we may become a blessing to those in need. We will get to covetousness below in the tenth commandment, but I want to mention here that we live in a greedy world, and our Father wants us to manage money in the direct opposite fashion.

This is how you combat the spirit of stealing or theft: "And if any man will sue thee at the law, and take away thy coat, let him have thy cloak also" (Matthew 5:40).

Here Jesus is preaching His famous sermon on the mount. He is teaching how to love your enemies and a new way of thinking in a world full of vengeance. Here He shows how a bad person could unjustly win a lawsuit, essentially stealing your coat. Your reaction should be to give him your cloak as well, showing love as opposed to hatred. Sound familiar?

Managing God's resources with His wisdom goes against our default thoughts. Remember, His ways are certainly not our ways.

THOU SHALT NOT BEAR FALSE WITNESS

[Exodus 20:16] Everything from "The Lord detest lying lips" to "worthless and wicked," the Bible is very clear that God does not like lying. Conversely, God loves the upright and honest, calling them trustworthy and righteous. If you were employing a manager, which one would you hire, the liar or the truth-teller?

In an article by Influencive, the author writes, "In the business world, there is sometimes a mindset that says small lies—so-called white lies—are acceptable if they are well intentioned or push you toward a goal. It's a 'the ends justify the means' mentality, and it's more widely-accepted than most people realize. However, lying in the workplace can generate very negative effects."[8]

Below, I summarize the outcomes of lying in the workplace found by this study:

- *It erodes the trust your employees have in you.*
- *It can affect your ability to win over clients and investors.*
- *Dishonesty actually makes you less intelligent in the moment, and thus less able to make moral decisions—and that can hurt you in almost any area of your business.*
- *But never fear. You know God has a reward for those who are honest.*
- *When employees see their leaders are honest, it encourages them to be honest, too.*
- *Honesty attracts new clients who want trustworthy business partners.*
- *Potential clients or partners appreciate it and will reward you with their business.*
- *Your confidence in what you say will shine through and have a positive impact, improving your mental health and critical thinking skills.*

Reinforced under the New Covenant: "Wherefore putting away lying, speak every man truth with his

There is an

abundance of blessing

for those who are

honest.

neighbour: for we are members one of another" (Ephesians 4:25).

Liars usually believe they have gotten away with their false narrative, but the Holy Spirit knows. As we see in Acts Chapter 5, Ananias and Sapphira lied to the church concerning a financial transaction. It did not end well. Being honest in all our business dealing is of paramount importance. Corporations that have collapsed because of fraud and false or inappropriate accounting are far too common today.

Don't get caught up in lying to "get ahead," because the outcome is never what it seems. When I hear of cases where someone has moved money to qualify for government benefits, or has lied about charitable contributions, I can identify this person's financial, mental, and spiritual state. They are broke and broken; and I know the cure.

There is an abundance of blessing for being honest. The cliché is right after all: honesty is the best policy.

THOU SHALT NOT COVET

[Exodus 20:17] Coveting is many times defined as "yearning." This word evokes a passionate picture of wanting something, but in this case that something is not earned or merited. Covetousness is a very dangerous evil and leads to great greed that stunts financial growth.

All of these financial sins are associated with the spirit of mammon, which in *Biblical Faith Meets Financial Strategy* I call, "financial heart disease." Covetousness is especially linked to your financial heart and is extremely poisonous. Jesus lists it among other issues which come from deep within a wicked heart: "For from within, out of the heart of men, proceed evil thoughts, adulteries, fornications, murders, thefts, **covetousness**, wickedness, deceit, lasciviousness, an evil eye, blasphemy, pride, foolishness: all these evil things come from within, and defile the man" (Mark 7:21-23).

You will find jealousy and envy tightly intertwined with covetousness. If you have the feeling of missing out on something because of someone else's experience, event, or possession, beware. Check your heart before the disease spreads.

Reinforced under the New Covenant: Have nothing to do with "...fornication, uncleanness, inordinate affection, evil concupiscence, and **covetousness**, which is idolatry" (Colossians 3:5).

To reaffirm how dangerous covetousness is, desiring your neighbor's possessions is listed together with these other sins. This should make you double check your motives and longings in life.

Social media is a huge driver for deceiving you into this trap. Perfect pictures and videos feed an endless scrolling mobile phone, giving you a rush of godless thoughts and feelings for things and places God does not intend for you to have or experience. Don't get caught up in this net of concupiscence. It doesn't mean you will never have or experience what you see, only that now may not be the time. Doom scrolling only ends up leading to mismanagement of money by going down the wrong path.

If your money management feels stuck, fix your financial focus and make sure there is no sign of covetousness. Then apply the antidotes of obedience, reverence, and love.

But wait, there's more …

The Greatest Commandments

Let's look closely at the two foundational commandments given by Jesus. These two commandments are not add-ons to the ten, but support the ten.

In Matthew 22, a lawyer approached Jesus to test Him with this question: "Which is the great commandment in the law?" And, of course, Jesus gave him even more than he asked for, providing two commandments.

Jesus said to him, "'You shall love the Lord your God with all your heart, with all your soul, and with all your mind.' This is the first and great commandment. And the second is like it: 'You shall love your neighbor as yourself.'

On these two commandments hang all the Law and the Prophets." (Matthew 22:37-40)

As you now see, "love" is at the intersection of God's ownership and money management. If you love God with all your heart, soul, and mind, your actions are going to speak far louder than words.

Do you believe God created and owns everything? That includes the job you have, the talent you possess, the money you manage, your family and relationships—your entire life. If you believe that, does your life reflect that honor and love you have for Him?

There is an easy way to find out. Do you have any other god before Him? Do you take His name in vain? Is your faith in graven images? Are you taking that day of rest He confirmed from the beginning? These four commandments sit on top of the first and greatest commandment.

If you love your neighbor, and all others, as yourself, your actions will not lie. The last half of the ten commandments are repeated verbatim in Romans 13:9, and then they are summed up with these seven words: "Thou shalt love thy neighbour as thyself."

Just quiz yourself. Do you honor your father, mother and other authorities in your life? Have you been hateful and unkind to others? Is there any sign of financial infidelity in your life? Have you taken the Lord's portion or someone else's possessions that don't belong to you? Have you falsified a financial document? Do you want what someone else has, though you have not earned it, neither is it the right timing in your life?

If you follow these two great commandments, on which the ten hang, every principle in the Bible will be a natural part of your life. Yes, these commandments convict, but they are there to direct you towards great blessing. When you love, love is reciprocated.

In a sermon by Nick Strobel, he says, "We should notice that the Ten Commandments are given after God has delivered the Hebrew people from slavery and the tyranny of the world power of that time. God's grace came *first*. Now God gives to the people through Moses the law, the teaching, the 'torah' that they will need in their new lives in freedom."[1] They viewed it as a guideline to live a successful life imparted in the same way that a father would instruct his child.

> *My child, listen when your father corrects you. Don't neglect your mother's instruction. What you learn from them will crown you with grace and be a chain of honor around your neck (Proverbs 1:8-9 NLT).*

Strobel continues by showing how the Hebrews saw the blessing of the Ten Commandments. They saw the Love of God through these instructions instead of only law. By contrast, most Christians see only rules.

So, as you continue to study the scriptures and apply them to your working, learning and managing of money, I challenge you to view the Ten Commandments from the perspective of love so that you can be the best steward possible and realize real financial freedom. God, the Owner, is the same yesterday, today, and forever; if He meant these words then, He means them now. Apply God's Wisdom to your management of God's Wealth, and you will certainly succeed.

The place where ownership and management intersect is critically important. Take your job seriously, and the reward will be more than you could ever imagine. There will be nothing like hearing those words, "Well done good and faithful steward!"

Free Resources

To help you Zero In on the INTERSECTION where God's Wealth meets God's Wisdom, download the free resources from the INTERSECTION Resource Page:

intersection.zeroinfinancial.com

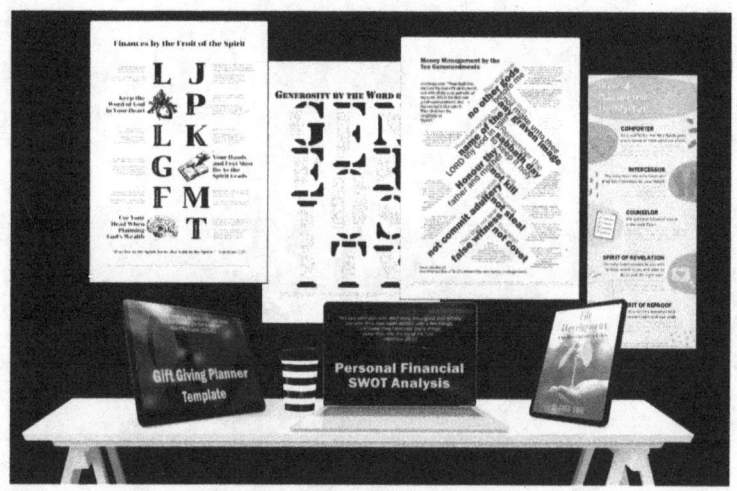

- **BOOK:** Life Development—A New Believer's Guide to Growing in Christ

- **INFOGRAPHIC:** Financial Guidance from the Holy Spirit

- **POSTER:** Finances by the Fruit of the Spirit

- **WORKBOOK:** Personal Financial SWOT Analysis

- **POSTER:** Money Management by the Ten Commandments

- **WORKBOOK:** Gift Giving Planner Template

- **POSTER:** Generosity by the Word of God

Thank You!

To all those who have been so generous to financially support the creation of this book series, I am so thankful. You helped bring INTERSECTION to fruition.

Forward Church Myrtle Beach

Kuba Wyrobek

Clovers & Val McWilliams

Carlos & Maria Correa

Ellie Markova

Anton & Aleksandra Zhloba

Pastor Chris, Heather, & Nelson Honeycutt

Dr. Anthony Jenkins

Pastor Allen & Debbie Causey

D.S. & Stella Wilson

D. Greg & Susie Ebie

David & Kelly Franco

Nicholas Ryan Rendleman

Kaffa Morales

Scott Petrarca

Marcos & Mireya Bernal

Angel Christopher

Pastor Steve & Jessica Mueller

Nick Kolovos

Anibal & Joelia Maldonado

David Gumins

J. Varghese

Linda Ostrowski

Steve & Traci Hickman

Richard L. Dobbins, Jr.

Pastor Edgar & Christie Rivas

Christian Baird

John Kuntharayil

Vuong Dinh

Chaplain James F. Burling

Adele van der Lecq

Edgar Rios

Note from the Author: Reviews are gold to authors! If you have enjoyed this book, would you consider reviewing it on your favorite book retailer's website? Thank you!

Notes

Chapter One: The Creation

[1] Isaacson, Walter. Steve Jobs. New York: Simon & Schuster, 2011
[2] McWilliams, Johnny. Biblical Faith Meets Financial Strategy. 2nd ed.
INTERSECTION - Where God's Wealth Meets God's Wisdom 1. Myrtle Beach, South Carolina: Zero In Financial Press, 2022

Chapter Two: The Law

[1] Anchorsaway. "Do Christians Have a Choice or Is God a Dictator?" Accessed August 8, 2021. https://anchorsaway.org/do-christians-have-a-choice-or-is-god-a-dictator/
[2] Williams, Mark. "Workplace Rules For Business Owners & Employees." Wolters Kluwer, July 6, 2021. https://www.wolterskluwer.com/en/expert-insights/workplace-rules-for-business-owners-and-employees
[3] Lee, Katherine. "Surprising Reasons Why We Need to Discipline Children." Verywell Family, October 1, 2020. https://www.verywellfamily.com/surprising-reasons-why-we-need-to-discipline-children-620115
[4] Knowing Jesus. "What Does Romans 3:31 Mean?" Accessed January 9, 2021. https://dailyverse.knowing-jesus.com/romans-3-31
[5] McWilliams, Johnny. "Dedicating Your Life to Jesus." Zero In Financial. Accessed January 15, 2022. https://zeroinfinancial.com/salvation/
[6] Hancock, Harold. "Are We Under The Ten Commandments, Today?" Timberland Drive. Accessed January 1, 2022. https://www.timberlandchurch.org/articles/are-we-under-the-ten-commandments-today
[7] McWilliams, Johnny. "Zero In Financial Press | INTERSECTION." Zero In Financial. Accessed April 4, 2020. https://zeroinfinancial.com/press/intersection
[8] Oxford Advanced American Dictionary. "Alms | Definition," January 25, 2020. https://www.oxfordlearnersdictionaries.com/us/definition/english/alms

Chapter Three: The Redemption

[1] Sowell, Thomas. "Random Thoughts." Jewish World Review, August 11, 2009. https://jewishworldreview.com/cols/sowell081109.php3

Chapter Four: What Tithing Is and Is Not

[1] McWilliams, Johnny. Biblical Faith Meets Financial Strategy. 2nd ed.
INTERSECTION - Where God's Wealth Meets God's Wisdom 1. Myrtle Beach, South Carolina: Zero In Financial Press, 2022.
[2] Dictionary, Merriam-Webster. "Tithe | Definition." Merriam-Webster.com. Accessed July 30, 2021. https://www.merriam-webster.com/dictionary/tithe
[3] McWilliams, Johnny. "Create a Powerful Budget – Prioritize Your OUTGO." Zero In Financial, January 21, 2021. https://zeroinfinancial.com/create-a-powerful-budget-prioritize-your-outgo/

Chapter Five: Protection & Prosperity

[1] Britannica, The Editors of Encyclopaedia. "Cornerstone | Definition." Encyclopedia Britannica, August 14, 2008. https://www.britannica.com/technology/cornerstone
[2] Britannica, The Editors of Encyclopaedia. "Pillar | Definition." Encyclopedia Britannica, December 13, 2010. https://www.britannica.com/technology/pillar
[3] Morris, Robert. The Blessed Life. Ventura, California: Regal, 2009

Chapter Six: God's Examples

[1] Toledo, Pastor Al. "Like a Tree." Chicago Tabernacle, February 11, 2018. https://www.chicagotabernacle.org/series/like-a-tree/

[2] Morris, Robert. The Blessed Life. Ventura, California: Regal, 2009

[3] Danker, Frederick W., Walter Bauer, and William Arndt. A Greek-English Lexicon of the New Testament and Other Early Christian Literature. 3rd ed. Chicago: University of Chicago Press, 2001

Chapter Seven: Working

[1] Merriam-Webster. "Steward | Definition," January 5, 2020. https://www.merriam-webster.com/dictionary/steward

[2] Hyatt, Michael S., and Megan Hyatt Miller. Win at Work and Succeed at Life: 5 Principles to Free Yourself From the Cult of Overwork. Grand Rapids, Michigan: Baker Books, a division of Baker Publishing Group, 2021

[3] Sams, Angela. "The Consequences of Not Working." MCN | Medical Consultants Network, February 5, 2016. https://mcn.com/2016/02/05/the-consequences-of-not-working/

[4] Swain, Dr Carol. "From Rural Poverty to the Ivy League." 1776 Unites | Uplifting Everyday Americans, July 20, 2020. https://1776unites.com/essays/from-rural-poverty-to-ivy-league-professor-carol-swains-life-lessons/

[5] Payne, Kevin. "The Simple Guide To Find Your God Given Purpose In Life." Kevin T Payne, May 1, 2018. https://www.kevintpayne.com/the-simple-guide-to-find-your-god-given-purpose-in-life/

[6] McWilliams, Johnny. Biblical Faith Meets Financial Strategy. 2nd ed. INTERSECTION - Where God's Wealth Meets God's Wisdom 1. Myrtle Beach, South Carolina: Zero In Financial Press, 2022

Chapter Eight: Learning

[1] Encyclopedia.com. "Atrophy | Definition," May 14, 2018. https://www.encyclopedia.com/medicine/diseases-and-conditions/pathology/atrophy

[2] Yirka, Bob. "Researchers Find IQ Scores Dropping since the 1970s." Medical Xpress, June 12, 2018. https://medicalxpress.com/news/2018-06-iq-scores-1970s.html

[3] Gray, Richard. "British Teenagers Have Lower IQs than Their Counterparts Did 30 Years Ago." The Telegraph, February 7, 2009. https://www.telegraph.co.uk/education/educationnews/4548943/British-teenagers-have-lower-IQs-than-their-counterparts-did-30-years-ago.html

[4] National Financial Educators Council. "National Financial Capability Test: Financial Capability Quiz." Accessed September 4, 2021. https://www.financialeducatorscouncil.org/national-financial-capability-test/

[5] McWilliams, Johnny. "Zero In Financial Press | INTERSECTION." Zero In Financial. Accessed April 4, 2020. https://zeroinfinancial.com/press/intersection

[6] Federal Reserve Bank of New York. "The Labor Market for Recent College Graduates." Accessed March 2, 2021. https://www.newyorkfed.org/research/college-labor-market

[7] Moawad M.D., Heidi. "Benefits of Reading Books: How It Can Positively Affect Your Life." Healthline, October 15, 2019. https://www.healthline.com/health/benefits-of-reading-books

Chapter Nine: Managing

[1] McWilliams, Johnny. Biblical Faith Meets Financial Strategy. 2nd ed. INTERSECTION - Where God's Wealth Meets God's Wisdom 1. Myrtle Beach, South Carolina: Zero In Financial Press, 2022

[2] The Christian Broadcasting Network. "Goodbye to Bad Attitudes," October 16, 2013. https://www1.cbn.com/family/goodbye-to-bad-attitudes

[3] Henry, Matthew. Matthew Henry's Commentary on the Whole Bible: Complete and Unabridged. Carol Stream, Illinois: Tyndale House Publishers, 2009

[4] McWilliams, Johnny. "Zero In Financial Press | INTERSECTION." Zero In Financial. Accessed April 4, 2020. https://zeroinfinancial.com/press/intersection

[5] McWilliams, Johnny. Divine Provision Meets Generosity Planning. INTERSECTION - Where God's Wealth Meets God's Wisdom 1. Myrtle Beach, South Carolina: Zero In Financial Press, 2022

Chapter Ten: Money Management by The Ten Commandments

[1] Prager, Dennis. The Ten Commandments: Still the Best Moral Code. Washington DC: Regnery Publishing, 2015

[2] Petruzzello, Melissa. "Mammon | Definition." Encyclopedia Britannica, September 8, 2020. https://www.britannica.com/topic/mammon

[3] ActiveChristianity. "Do You Worship the Creator or Just the Creation?," September 17, 2018. https://activechristianity.org/god-the-creator-of-all-things

[4] Bible History. "The Worship of Baal." Accessed July 2, 2020. https://bible-history.com/resource/the-worship-of-baal

[5] Bridges, Charles, and George Frederick Santa. A Modern Study in the Book of Proverbs. Milford, Michigan: Mott Media, 1978

[6] Writing Explained. "What Does Cheaters Never Prosper Mean?" Accessed October 10, 2021. https://writingexplained.org/idiom-dictionary/cheaters-never-prosper

[7] Cruze, Rachel. "Overcoming Financial Infidelity." Ramsey Solutions, September 27, 2021. https://www.ramseysolutions.com/relationships/overcoming-financial-infidelity

[8] Silva, Los. "The Real Benefits of Honesty in the Workplace." Influencive, February 5, 2017. https://www.influencive.com/real-benefits-honesty-workplace/

Conclusion: The Greatest Commandments

[1] Strobel, Nick. "The Blessing Of and From the Ten Commandments." Wesley Bakersfield, October 5, 2008. https://www.wesleybakersfield.org/sermons/05oct08-strobel.htm

About the Author

Johnny McWilliams, founder of Zero In Financial LLC, guides his students, customers, and clients as they RECOVER from past money mistakes, GROW your present pocketbook position, and ZERO IN on your future financial fortune, ultimately leaving a lasting legacy of love. After working as a tax preparer, dissecting the details of credit scoring and reporting, passing various exams and licensure, including Series 7, Series 66, life & health insurance, and real estate broker, Johnny realized the average American's need for financial coaching, education, and inspiration.

Once Johnny completed ten years of enlistment in the United States Navy, graduated with a Master of Business Administration, worked as a property & casualty insurance consultant, and became certified as a Ramsey Solutions Master Financial Coach, he began guiding individuals and families to Zero In on their financial target.

Johnny and his wife, Christine, have been married for over twelve years, and they are blessed with one married son, one married daughter, and no grandchildren yet.